What The Hell Do I Do Now?

A Professionals' Guide
to a Meaningful Retirement

R. Dean White

DISCLAIMER

This book details the author's personal experiences with and opinions about the challenges of retirement. The author is not a licensed psychologist, physician or counselor.

The author and publisher are providing this book and its contents on an "as is" basis and make no representations or warranties of any kind with respect to this book or its contents. The author and publisher disclaim all such representations and warranties, including for example warranties of merchantability and personal, medical, psychological or financial advice for a particular purpose. In addition, the author and publisher do not represent or warrant that the information accessible via this book is accurate, complete or current.

The statements made about products and services have not been evaluated by the U.S. government. Please consult with your own legal or accounting professional regarding the suggestions and recommendations made in this book.

Except as specifically stated in this book, neither the author or publisher, nor any authors, contributors, or other representatives will be liable for damages arising out of or in connection with the use of this book. This is a comprehensive limitation of liability that applies to all damages of any kind, including (without limitation) compensatory; direct, indirect or consequential damages; loss of data, income or profit; loss of or damage to property and claims of third parties.

You understand that this book is not intended as a substitute for consultation with a licensed medical, legal or accounting professional. Before you begin any change your lifestyle in any way, you will consult a licensed professional to ensure that you are doing what's best for your situation.

This book provides content related to psychological, medical and financial topics. As such, use of this book implies your acceptance of this disclaimer.

This book is dedicated to my best friend and wife, Vickie

And

Our three daughters, Jennifer, Lindsay and Shannon

Acknowledgements

First and foremost, I have to thank Elizabeth C Jones, my editor, for correcting my musings, adding insights and wisdom, and keeping me focused to make this book relevant and meaningful. Special thanks are in order for Bob Karper, who has challenged me all along the way and went to work writing to help me make a point. Saundra Marling was very helpful in sharing her wisdom dealing with retirement, and Dave Diesslin was very instructive in his discussion about the aspects of financial health. I appreciate the candor and introspection of all my interviewees and friends. Harry Karegeannes, Vern Oechsle, Ron Stegal, Lou Hendrickx, Jim Rickman, Jim Schierling, Aubrey and Barbara Guthrie, Norb Walter and Bob Thompson all contributed immensely to the process.

I have attempted to provide extensive footnotes and references for my thoughts and recommendations, and I truly thank all the researchers, writers, and authors who add to the ever expanding body of knowledge. I would especially like to thank Therese Borchan for her permission to use her "Twelve Ways to be Thankful". Most of all I thank, Vickie White, my wife of 42 years, who was my first proof reader and continued to give me advice all along the way.

Table of Contents

Chapter Summaries xiii

Introduction 1

Chapter One - CHANGE/RELEVANCE 5

    A. My Story 7

    B. Ron's Story 12

    C. Relevance is Relative 16

Chapter Two - BALANCE/PERSPECTIVE 21

    A. Creating Balance 24

    B. Work 25

    C. The second career 26

    D. Volunteering 33

    E. Family 35

    F. Recreation 39

    G. Spirituality 40

    H. Lou's Story: Finding Balance 45

Chapter Three - SOLITUDE/BOREDOM 49

A. The Sunny Side of Solitude 51

B. Leave your legacy..55

C. The Dark Side of Solitude..58

Chapter Four - AGING/HEALTH 67

A. The Science Behind Exercise, Diet, and Sleep for the Chronologically Impaired..69

B. Holding Off the Grim Reaper with Exercise 74

C. Stop Eating Pimento Loaf and Twinkies...................81

D. Get Your Beauty Sleep...86

E. Where Did I Put My Keys?..89

Chapter Five - MENTORSHIP/LEADERSHIP 97

A. Anyone Can Be a Mentor...98

B. Pay it Forward..101

C. Honesty, Trust, Positive Vision, and Emotional Intelligence ...103

D. Honesty and Trust 104

E. Positive Vision 107

F. Emotional Intelligence 108

G. Jim Rickman's Story: Mentoring the Next Generation............112

H. Jim Schierling's Story: Teaching Grace 114

Chapter Six - THANKFULNESS/APOLOGY 117

A. Homework: Make a Happy List 126

B. Caring for Aging Parents: The Ultimate Thank You 127

C. Where Will Mom and Dad Live?.............................129

D. Who Will Pay for Mom and Dad's Needs? 131

E. How Will I Take Care of Myself? 133

F. Speak Now or Forever Hold your Peace: Learning to
Apologize 134

G. Norb's Story: The Joy of Giving 142

Chapter Seven - LEGACY/LEFTOVERS 145

A. Consider Your Legacy 146

B. Exercises to Help you Find Your Personal Legacy...................152

C. Write Your Own Obituary:....................................152

D. Get Back to Your Roots.......................................153

E. Vern's Story: Balancing the Karmic Scales by Creating a New
Legacy 155

F. There are no luggage racks on hearses........................157

Chapter Eight - PERSONAL REFLECTIONS..................................... **161**

    A. Harry Karegeannes' Story 161

    B. Bob Karper's Story 174

    C. Bob Thompson's story 181

Chapter Nine - FICTION, FACTS, AND FINANCES **187**

    A. Making Money without an Income 189

    B. Organizing your Assets..190

    C. Choosing an Advisory Firm.....................................193

    D. Going it Alone 196

Chapter Ten - PIDDLING, POTHOLES, AND PEARLS **201**

    A. Piddle Away a Few Hours a Week 202

    B. Avoid Potholes 203

    C. Aubrey and Barbara Guthrie's Story: Sharing Pearls of
       Wisdom...205

    D. You Can't Get a Butterfly by Stapling Wings to a Worm 208

    E. Finding Pearls 209

Chapter Summaries

Chapter One: Change and Relevance

Change is unavoidable, but daunting at times. Change should be embraced as an opportunity for the individual who is retiring. My story of involuntary change at the age of 55 illustrates that the future can be frightening but rewarding. Ron Stegal, who founded Biz Mart and Pet Smart, describes how difficult it was for him to retire and how he finally found his niche. All of us want to stay relevant and have meaningful lives even after we give up our day jobs.

Chapter Two: Balance and Perspective

Balance is critical in retirement. Many successful professionals and executives are not familiar with the concept of balance. Balancing work, family, recreation, and spiritual pursuits is the key to a happy and successful retirement. Opportunities for the work portion of the equation are endless, from volunteering to pursuing that long-lost dream. Lou Hendrickx, a former CIA division chief, shares his successful pursuit of balance.

Chapter Three: Solitude and Boredom

Solitude can be a great blessing, but unless it is nourished, it can become a curse. Many highly functioning individuals have not learned to be comfortable alone. Boredom may be another word for lazy, but it needs to be recognized for what it is and not allowed to turn into depression. Many life changes, including retirement, can initiate a depressive episode. It is critical that an individual experiencing depressive thoughts recognizes it and seeks professional help.

Chapter Four: Aging and Health

The two most dreaded words in the English language are "diet" and "exercise." Healthy habits will allow a retiree to enjoy and prolong his or her future. The aspects of aging and cognitive decline are something we all want to avoid; but of course, we all must learn to deal with them. Strategies for postponing the effects of aging through diet, exercise, and good sleep patterns are detailed with the research to support them. Robert Karper, MD, helps explain the science behind the recommendations.

Chapter Five: Mentorship and Leadership

Many professionals and executives have highly developed skills in leadership, mentorship, and management. These are all critical skills in retirement and can be leveraged second and third careers, as well as volunteering pursuits. Honesty, forward and positive vision, and emotional intelligence are applicable in retirement. An engineer and a pastor illustrate the principles of each.

Chapter Six: Thankfulness and Apology

The importance of being thankful is explained both from a psychological and physical sense. Therese Borchan explains the art of thankfulness and the many ways to incorporate it into one's daily life. The ultimate thank you may be taking care of aging parents, and we cover multiple aspects of this often difficult responsibility. The art of apology is also critical to enjoying retirement, as the psychological benefits of tying off loose ends and healing are profound.

Chapter Seven: Legacy and Leftovers

Leaving a legacy may not be the accolades, positions, and awards one earned during a fruitful career. Rather, one's legacy may be forged during retirement. This chapter encourages readers to think about what they would like their obituaries to say. Vern Oechsle, a Harvard MBA, discusses his legacy. Leftovers refer to all that junk we leave behind and ways to meaningfully distribute it before it is too late to decide. There are no luggage racks on hearses.

Chapter Eight: Personal Reflections

This is the story of three highly accomplished individuals. One is a retired major general in the U.S. Army one is a clinical pathologist and the third is retired structural engineer. Their trials, tribulations, planning, insights, disappointments, and ultimately success in retirement are enlightening and instructive.

Chapter Nine: Fiction, Facts, and Finances

This is not a financial guide, but rather the fuel that drives readers to think deeply about their financial wellbeing. Dave Diesslin, MBA, a certified financial planner, explains the concepts and theories behind successful retirement from a money management viewpoint. He discusses how to choose a financial advisor and how to manage finances on your own.

Chapter Ten: Piddling, Potholes and Pearls

This chapter glues the rest of the book together. It discusses the importance of piddling to the retiree. It also discusses potholes, those diversions and hazards that sometimes show up in the roads we travel. Sometimes we hit them and sometimes we avoid them, but the trick is not to let them derail our journey. Pearls are nuggets of information or advice worth keeping. A physician and his PhD wife share their recommendations, which are true pearls.

Introduction

"We don't care what you used to do, we don't care how much money you have, and we don't want to hear anything about your health. Other than that, you can talk about anything."

~Said to the newcomer to the golf foursome at a retirement community in East Texas

This book is a guide for baby boomers who are about to or have already retired from an all-consuming profession and are terrified. They wake up in the mornings with the vast expanse of the day ahead of them and wonder, "What the hell do I do with myself now?"

Retirement, for the purpose of this book, is not about buying a condo in South Florida, drinking gin, and playing golf. It is a major life change, much like getting married or having children. For individuals, such as physicians, lawyers, executives, and others with high-demand professions, retirement (as frightening as it is) is an opportunity to do something else equally as meaningful as the jobs they previously held.

For many years now, I've worked with physicians who face physical and cognitive decline that forces them to retire sooner than they had planned, and they need guidance. These individuals spent years in school training for their chosen profession, performed at a high level for many more years, and can be described as overachievers. They now must ask themselves "What do I do now?"

I am a retired oral and maxillofacial surgeon who had to stop practicing at age 55 due to a neurological disorder. Therefore, I wrote this book based on personal experience. I also conducted research and interviewed others who have retired successfully. For this book, I interviewed physicians, engineers, a pastor, a major general, a CIA division chief, a career counselor, a financial advisor, a nurse and educator, and several CEOs and corporate executives for their perspectives, insight, and advice.

Retirement is naturally a challenge when a highly trained individual gets his or her gold watch and walking papers in return for decades of service. This book will explain why it is what we learn after we know it all that really counts. Many will view this discussion as just common sense, but common sense is illusive at times. We will explore the nature of change, balance, aging, health, boredom, thankfulness, mentoring, solitude, freedom, and legacy, and the art of piddling.

I hope this book will help you enter this next phase of your life with positive expectations of what will become the best part of your life.

Chapter One
CHANGE/RELEVANCE

"Each segment of the journey of life should be embraced fully and actively, ever mindful, however, that this is a continuous passage with new challenges (and opportunities). It is fair to reminisce about what has gone before, but it is neither helpful nor realistic to fight the ongoing stream, attempting to remain fixed in one area beyond one's allotted time."

Richard Rovit, MD[1]

People change. Period. We change mentally, cognitively, and physically regardless of all our efforts otherwise. Our values, goals, and interests change. We make new friends, and old friends die. Our children move away,

---

1 Rovit, Richard. "To everything there is a season and a time to every purpose: retirement of the neurosurgeon." *Journal of Neurosurgery*; 100:1123-1129.

taking our grandchildren with them. We eventually have to bury our only true fans, our parents. It's not always easy, but sometimes it's for the best.

But just because we change doesn't mean we simultaneously become irrelevant. We grow up, we grow old, but we don't have to get left behind. Eric Shinseki, retired United States Army four-star general and current United States Secretary of Veterans Affairs, said it best: "If you think you hate change, you are really going to hate being irrelevant."

Many have spent an entire lifetime, sometimes at the expense of their own health and relationships, becoming excellent in a particular vocation or endeavor, only to be told by someone else or to realize for them that it is time to retire. Rather than letting retirement stagnate you, it's important to learn how to stay relevant, engaged, active, and interested each and every day you are given.

I will tell my story of change along with many others that were kind enough to share with me their thoughts and experiences when they retired.

A. My Story

At the age of 55, I was at the top of my game and making more money than I deserved. I enjoyed my hard-earned reputation for being able to reconstruct complex facial deformities that were a result of severe temporomandibular joint disease. These procedures required four to six hours at an operating room table, usually standing in one position working through small incisions. Success and failure were only millimeters apart.

At the age of 53, I noticed that my hands were numb when I woke up in the morning and many times during long surgical procedures I was performing. After several consultations and electromyography, my physician determined that I had developed significant carpal tunnel disease that required surgical intervention on both hands. I elected to have both hands corrected at the same time and recovered quickly. I was back operating within a month and thought I was home free. I was wrong.

A year and a half later, I started noticing the same numbness I had experienced previously along with a loss of motor function. I was dropping instruments, my hands cramped, and I experienced a general lack of feeling in my fingers and hands. After magnetic resonance imaging, myelograms, electromyography, and physical examinations, I learned that the symptoms were caused by rather significant cervical spondylosis and spinal cord atrophy. The surgeons offered to intervene surgically but said the symptoms would remain and could become worse after the intervention. I was told by three neurosurgeons that I should probably quit practicing as an oral and maxillofacial surgeon so that I did not harm any patients. I was also told that if I continued to damage my neck, I would not be able to button my own shirts in a few short years. I had a doctorate and a master degree, but no undergraduate degree, and no real skills other than my surgical ones. Change was staring me in the face.

What transpired from there was both unintended and rewarding. I had just completed a two-year stint as chief of the medical staff at the hospital where I had practiced for 30 years, and hospital administration offered me a part-time job as a medical staff advisor. The medical staff advisor position was created specifically for me, and I got to write a new job description (for the most part). I was charged with getting the administration, the physician staff, and the nursing staff on the same page. (One might think that physicians, nurses, and administration already work on the same page, but, quite frankly, they don't.) As Atul Gawande, MD, noted surgeon and author, stated in his graduation speech to the Harvard Medical School students in 2011, "We train, hire, and pay doctors to be cowboys. But its pit crews people need." I had my work cut out for me.

I began my tenure as medical staff advisor by overseeing several committees charged with managing both the clinical and behavioral aspects of the medical staff. I began to work with physicians who had anger management issues, alcohol and drugs dependency, communication deficits, and physical and cognitive symptoms due to aging. I did not have a background in psychology, communication, or management, but I learned from experience and had some successes and failures along the way.

As administrators, physicians, nurses, and management personnel changed, my job description changed. Medical staff and hospital leaders began asking me to share my experiences with groups of medical staff professionals, physician leaders, and administrative leaders in other hospitals. This became an interesting way to see many parts of the country, visit with some engaging people, and learn from listening. The more people heard me speak, the more I was asked to speak, and I was encouraged to develop a Web site. One company that I spoke for a few times asked me to write a book on managing disruptive and impaired physicians followed by another book on the principles of medical staff leadership. At this point, I am way out of my comfort zone of what I used to do, but I am having a great time, making a little money, and feeling like I have found relevance in a whole new way.

With my new path ahead of me, the Santé Center for Healing, which specializes in helping professionals with alcohol, drug, and sex addictions, asked me to join the faculty of a course for physicians and other professionals who have boundary issues. Most of the participants are required by their state regulatory agencies to take the courses; if they fail to do so, they risk losing their practice licenses or position of authority. The courses are co-sponsored by Southwestern Medical School in Dallas and the Santé Center for Healing. The directors of these continuing medical education courses continue to give me the responsibility of interacting with these individuals, helping them understand empathy, ethics, professionalism, and boundaries. I help them create strategies that enable them to remain productive members of their professions.

I'll be the first to say that they don't teach these skills in dental school. Helping these individuals overcome their addictions and boundary issues became a highlight of my third career. One of the participants, a psychiatrist, was a sex and drug addict, and he was interested in my role as an educator and mentor. He asked me how he might be able to start helping others with addictions, and one of the other participants said to him, "First you have to become an oral surgeon." The look on his face was priceless. It goes to show that although I didn't set out to be an educator and counselor for physicians with addictions, this is where my life has led me. In time, you may end up doing something you never imagined yourself doing and thoroughly enjoying it!

B. Ron's Story

Ron Stegal, retired business executive and entrepreneur summed up his attempts at retiring by saying "If I had failed as badly and as many times in my business career as I have in retiring, I would be broke." Ron tells his story:

Retirement for me has been more a process than an event. The first time I retired, I was the senior vice president of Radio Shack, where I had started right out of college as a sales trainee making $1.45 an hour. I moved up to store manager, district manager, regional manager, division vice president, and finally to senior vice president by the age of 39. I had always loved being out in the field with the stores and field managers, but after three years as senior vice president, I realized that I spent 90% of my time locked up in a conference room in executive meetings. The fun was gone, and the company was just so big (5,000 stores and dealers versus 500 the day I joined the company) that we were losing touch with the field and what made us the great company we had become. I decided that we had made enough money on our Tandy Corp. stock that I could retire, so I did.

The next three months were probably the best of my life. We moved up to our Cedar Creek Lake house with our two elementary school-age kids. We boated, jet skied, sailed, and just played for the whole summer. Unfortunately, August came and the kids were headed back to school in Arlington. I quickly realized that I might have retired but, but my family had not.

I rented a space in our family attorney's office, bought a big fancy desk, and went to work every morning to just sit there and read The Wall Street Journal—no calls, no visitors. I lasted at this miserable pace for a couple months and decided that I had to do something challenging. I contacted a group of venture capital companies and raised $8 million to start BizMart Office Product Stores. Over the next four years, we grew from one model store to 58 stores in 18 states. The company earned revenues of more than $300 million and became publicly traded on the NASDX exchange. At that point, I *was having the time of my life running and growing the company, until Kmart, which had started Office Max in the Ohio area and was about one-third of the size of BizMart, called and wanted to purchase the company. The venture capital guys were more than happy to sell, as they had made about eight times their money in four years. After selling BizMart, I was back out looking for something to keep me busy, so I convinced my old financial officer from Radio Shack to come out of retirement to start a venture capital investment firm called Arlington Equity Partners. We invested in a pet supply startup company in Atlanta. I, as nonexecutive chairman, and my partner, helped build a management team and grew the company over three years to more than 50 stores in six states and sold it to PetSmart. We then started a children's clothing and supply superstore concept in Texas, and again, as nonexecutive chairman, built a management team and opened a couple dozen stores. We were never able to get the revenue to make a profitable business venture, so we eventually closed the stores and company.*

After this failing venture, I decided that 50 was a good retirement age, so I again retired but continued to sit on four public company boards and one private company board. This worked out well for a while because I could stay about as busy as I wanted to be by working with the CEOs of the different companies without being tied down to a real schedule. This semiretirement lasted almost five years until my daughter and son-in-law graduated with their MBAs and wanted to start a business. At the time, I was not real keen on the idea of starting a new business, but I told them that if they would go out and get a couple years of real-world corporate experience, I would start thinking about and looking for possible opportunities so we could start something of our own.

Being that my wife, Cindy, and I are both avid Harley-Davidson riders, having traveled on bikes all over North America and Europe, we focused on the opportunity to open a new Harley-Davidson dealership in Denton County. My deal with the kids and the Harley-Davidson Motor Company was that I would come out of retirement and go back to work fulltime to get the business started. Once it was on its feet, I would again retire. My original time table was a couple of years; however, the business turned out to be a much larger opportunity than we could have ever expected. After the second year of operation, we had become one of the largest Harley-Davidson dealers in the United States. We bought out the oldest original Dallas dealership in Carrollton and proceeded to double the size of that dealership. Overall, it took us more than five years to get both dealerships completely debt free and performing with a stable staff so that Cindy and I could really move on. Now, I was pushing 60, and if we were going to get out there and enjoy "the good life," I had better get on with it before I was too old.

Cindy and I retired from the dealerships five years ago. We bought our yacht and have been cruising the Caribbean, Pacific, Atlantic, and Mediterranean seas for the past five years, spending about three weeks each month on the boat and one week a month at home seeing our six grandchildren that all live in the Dallas Fort-Worth area.

C. Relevance is Relative

Not everyone will have the expertise, courage, and entrepreneurial spirit that Ron has, but the fact remains that retiring is not about renting an office and reading *The Wall Street Journal*. It is about new ventures, new risks, and new goals. It may involve learning to fly a glider, getting a history degree and teaching at the local junior college, learning a foreign language, square dancing, or volunteering. The list is endless, and as you read the rest of the stories, I hope you will see the enormous benefits to your health and your cognitive abilities to chase the dream, fulfill your bucket list, and make a difference in the world. No one says on their deathbed, "I wish I had spent more time at the office."

I once had the opportunity to ask one of my daughters, who was 16 at the time, what she thought about the fact that all of the members of The American Board of Oral and Maxillofacial Surgeons had successful marriages. We were celebrating one of the couple's 25th wedding anniversary, and I asked all seven couples to tell everyone how long they had been married (the range was from 18 to 45 years). My daughter simply stated "successful people are successful at a lot of things." She's right.

If you were successful at your previous job, you will, after an adjustment period and exploration, be successful at retirement, too. People who have enjoyed their past accomplishments are ideally suited to enjoy the next set of goals. People naturally resist change and are afraid of the unknown; we are fearful of giving up the people or the profession by which we identified ourselves. This is a huge problem for people in high-profile or high-demand jobs, such as physicians. For many physicians, not being a doctor anymore is just not acceptable. Doctors spend their entire lives in pursuit of helping others, and once they retire, they must fill a void that has fed their egos and self-esteem for years. It's not easy. I still have vivid dreams of performing complex surgical procedures and wake up exhausted (the good thing is that I never have any complications!), and I have been retired from oral surgery over ten years.

To help you on your journey, I suggest finding a role model. Most of us learn by observation, yet, many of us lack a role model, someone who has accomplished what we are striving for in our retirement. Hearing a lecture or reading a book about retirement will not get the job done;

you must seek out someone you know and trust and find out what they have learned through the process of retiring. I hope the stories told here will help you on this journey, but it helps to find someone to chat with over coffee or beer.

If you have not yet retired, you may find it helpful to take more time off as your retirement approaches, if you can. This additional time will allow you to test the waters of other pursuits. Use your weekends and vacations to try another place to live, if moving to a different area is one of your goals. Take some non-credit college courses to explore other interests or join a social networking group dedicated to a hobby of your choice so you can meet new people and learn as you go. If you start exploring your interests before retirement, you won't wake up the day after your send-off party wondering what on earth you are going to do now.

Inevitably, you will struggle—maybe a lot, maybe a little. Either way, some days will get you down. You might feel useless or lost, and that is normal. These feelings are temporary, but more importantly, they are useful. Use them as a catalyst to jumpstart your search for your post-retirement identity. Take a rainy day to volunteer at a local soup kitchen or research a topic that excites you. Chances are you wasted little time on the job, so use that same resourcefulness to keep a forward momentum.

Keep in mind that as you become part of a new social group, your past, particularly your "Who's Who" write-up, is not relevant anymore. You may find that the sting of not being able to say "I'm a brain surgeon" at cocktail parties fades with time, and you're more proud of teaching your grandson how to throw a curveball than the thousands of surgeries you performed over the years. This isn't to say that the work you did previously isn't important, but you'll find that your priorities change. If you're feeling lost at sea, it may help to stay abreast of your field and keep in touch with old colleagues to help you feel connected as you make the transition into retirement.

The point of all of this, of course, is that change is inevitable and now is the time to embrace it and make it your own.

Chapter Two
BALANCE/PERSPECTIVE

"The best and safest thing is to keep a balance in your life, acknowledge the great powers around us and in us. If you can do that, and live that way, you are really a wise man."

Euripides

During my last year of dental school, a practicing dentist in Houston gave a guest lecture for our course on psychology. He was somewhat disheveled, had crooked teeth, and seemed to be old school. He told us that what he was going to say to us could be the difference between success and failure in our profession. We immediately thought he was going to speak about making money, growing a practice, adopting innovative ways to present treatment plans, and so forth. But what he said has stuck with me the last 45 years and is some of the best advice I have ever received. I should have seen it coming, because my own father was a master at it and consistent until he died at the age of 95. The guest lecturer told us to practice balance in our lives. The four elements he discussed (namely work, family, recreation, and spirituality) should be as close to equal as possible so that you do not tip the scales. Many highly functioning, type-A workaholics seem to neglect three of the four, and the carnage is evident in their personal lives and relationships. Even if you have previously lacked insight and commitment to balance, it becomes critical for your physical and mental health as you retire.

Balance can be viewed from many perspectives; it has a different meaning for everyone depending on personality. Your personality largely decides how you will cope with the change inherent in retirement. There are all sorts of personality profiles: Right brain/left brain, attachment templates, Type A/Type B, birth order, and so forth. To a large degree, they are variations of the same themes, so understanding the nuances of each personality scale aren't important. It is, however, important that you understand your own personality and how you tend to cope with change.

Saundra Marling, BA, MEd, MCC, LPC, explains in her book, *Boomers' Job Search Guide: You're Not Old You're Experienced* (Life Transition Consulting, 2006), that different personality types approach retirement differently. If you are right handed and you break your right hand, you have to use the unnatural hand to function. It is tiring and takes a great deal of mental and physical attention. The same is true for the extrovert who retires and comes home to solitude or the introvert who must seek companionship. There is value in seeking the unnatural preferences. The trick is for both introverts and extroverts to understand the stress involved in retirement and the strategies to cope. If you don't know how your personality measures up on any of the scales, don't worry. Simply ask yourself, "How do I recharge?" If sitting quietly reading a book recharges your batteries and a large cocktail party drains them, you are probably an introvert and may cope better with the increased time alone after retirement. If the opposite is true, and you feel revitalized after a party, then you are probably an extrovert and will require more external stimulation.

Both the retiree and his or her spouse may wish to seek counseling to make this transition go as smoothly as possible. A life change, such as retirement, can propel an extrovert into being introverted, and vice versa, and he or she may not understand how to deal with the transition.

A. Creating Balance

People struggle to find balance because it does not always come naturally. Saundra asks her clients to depict how they use their time with a pie chart (you can use a pie chart to illustrate how you use your money, as well, which is a real eye-opener). Many times, how people perceive they spend their time is far from reality. Putting a finite number on your work, recreation, family, spiritual or quiet time, etc., can be instructive on just how balanced (or unbalanced) you are and help you decide how you would like to change it going forward. If the majority of your pie chart is taken up by work, brainstorm strategies for spending more time with your family or spirituality.

As life circumstances change (and they will), balance will be in jeopardy. It is not a time for panic, just a time for self-reflection, self-assessment, and self-correction. You may find that you go through a transition period where you flounder a bit—you're not exactly sure where your life should go. Dedicate some time to long walks, car rides, or any other activity that allows you time to contemplate deeply. This time of reflection may help you find your new direction. Don't be embarrassed if you need professional to help balance the scales; talking it out with a professional counselor may be exactly what you need.

B. Work

The work part of the balance equation will mean different things to different people. It is unreasonable to assume that everyone will have the means to retire without conditions. Some may need to work to make ends meet, while others may want to work to make a little extra money to enjoy some of the finer things that the golden years have to offer. Others may simply want to work, whether it is at a paying job or a volunteer opportunity, such as helping children at a local school with remedial reading or wielding a saw and hammer for Habitat for Humanity. Some baby boomers may want to launch into a second or even third career. No matter why or where you work, work needs to be an integral part of your retirement plan if you are going to achieve balance.

C. The second career

Many of us will need a second or third career to satisfy a need to work and supply some additional income. The goal is to turn your passion into profit. The profit may be monetary or simple perks. My third career as a consultant teaching principles of medical staff leadership has taken me to some of the finer resorts in the country. The sponsoring organization always pays the expenses plus a stipend. If I go by myself, I make a profit. If, however, my wife accompanies me (which she often does), we do well to break even. The room is paid for, we use frequent flier miles or pay for her airfare upfront, and when we add a round of golf and a couple of nice meals, we come out about even. The cool thing is that we have had all-expense paid long weekends to the coast of Maine, New Hampshire, Massachusetts, Oregon, Florida, and California. So, I might not be raking in the big bucks, but I consider spending time with my wife and seeing the country a "profit."

A recent poll by Knowledge Networks in Palo Alto, Calif. found that 73% of baby boomers plan to work into retirement. Marc Freedman made the term "encore career" popular in his book *Encore: Finding Work That Matters in the Second Half of Life* (Public Affairs, 2008). As he describes it, an encore career is one that supplies an individual with income, but more importantly, a greater meaning and a chance to have a social impact. These are paid positions in various fields, including education, environment, health, government, social services, and non-profit.

In the *MetLife Foundation/Civic Ventures Encore Career Survey*, Freedman said: *What if, over time, 100,000 people interested in encore careers were persuaded to launch 10-year encore careers? That would mean one million years of service dedicated to areas like education, poverty, and the environment. What if we could persuade a million more to do so?*

Nicholas Kristoff, in his July 20, 2008 *New York Times* article "Geezers Doing Good," states:

The trend known as an encore career may become a substitute for retirement. If more people take on encore careers, the boomers who arrived on the scene by igniting a sexual revolution could leave by staging a give-back revolution. Boomers may just be remembered more for what they did in their 60s than for what they did in the sixties.

In his new book, *The Big Shift: Navigating the New Stage Beyond Midlife* (Public Affairs, 2011), Freedman states that people are working longer because they not only need the income, but they also want to find meaning in life through work. In 2012, Intel instituted an Encore Fellowship program, which matches interested workers with a non-profit organization where they work for a minimum of six months to a year. Intel provides a $25,000 stipend and health insurance coverage. Richard Taylor, Intel's vice president of human resources, said in a press release that the company isn't using the program to thin its ranks of older workers. Rather, the program is part of the company's basic philosophy of "allowing workers to retire with dignity."

Many boomers who are still working are trapped by the "golden collar": they make a good income with benefits but hate their jobs. So, when it is time to retire, why not follow your passion to make up for all of the years spent in a job you didn't absolutely love? The opportunities are only limited by your imagination. Consider going back to school to follow your dream; there is no age limit on education. If you have always liked decorating, retrain and become a home decorator or remodeling expert. If you like camping, hiking, and fishing, consider being a nature guide or working in a retail outlet where you interface with those that are looking for your expertise. You get to choose.

Contrary to what you may think, older workers are in great demand. Compared to their younger counterparts, they are more stable, more reliable, have fewer sick days, do not have to take care of children, do not get pregnant and need maternity leave, and many do not have to have health insurance or other benefits because they are already under Medicare and/or Medicaid. That makes baby boomers ideal employees. Most companies have a policy that if you work less than three days a week, you do not qualify for their benefits, therefore, you are a bargain! Law school and business schools are always looking for candidates, and age is not a factor.

Marling has spent her career counseling those who have to change positions or are being terminated or transferred to other positions. She has worked for JC Penney, Abbott Labs, Frito Lay, and several large governmental agencies as an independent contractor. When we discussed the title of this book, Marling said that immediately several types came to mind, mainly surgeons, engineers, and pilots. In her experience, individuals in these three professions have a tough time giving up their day jobs and not bringing home a list of things for everyone in the family to do. Thus, it behooves them and their families to find post-retirement work. As we discussed retirement, she spoke of how she evaluates individuals who are about to retire. She takes into consideration their personality, skill sets, values, and self-assessment evaluations based on the Meyers-Briggs Personality Inventory. In her book,

Marling suggests making a list of the skills you want to use in your next job, such as:

- Instructing
- Operating machines or equipment
- Calculating
- Researching
- Training
- Managing
- Analyzing
- Hiring
- Communicating
- Mentoring/helping
- Assembling/building
- Facilitating
- Planning
- Persuading
- Designing
- Speaking

It may also help to make a list of personal traits that will help you identify the type of candidate you will be for a future employer, such as:

- Loyal
- Reliable
- Efficient
- Self-starter
- Accurate
- Organized
- Thorough
- Flexible
- Sympathetic
- Outgoing
- Creative
- Versatile
- Energetic
- Sensitive
- Motivated
- People-oriented
- Conscientious
- Problem solver

- Ability to relate

D. Volunteering

If a second or third career isn't in your line of vision, consider volunteering. Volunteers are needed everywhere. Physicians can work in charity clinics sponsored by churches or communities. They can mentor and teach in programs such as Health Volunteers Overseas, Doctors Without Borders, Help the Children, and many others. Accountants can help local charities keep their records straight; engineers can help with environmental or local building projects; anyone can help with Habitat for Humanity or Meals on Wheels. Dentists can work on a volunteer basis locally, nationally, or internationally and never come close to fulfilling the need for services. Corporate executives can help with executive leadership for churches and local charities.

Volunteering can help a new retiree create balance in life. It can also help you find perspective. One great example of finding perspective is detailed in the book by Ron Hall and Denver Moore, *Same Kind as Different as Me*, in which Ron Hall, an international art dealer with an MBA, volunteers at the local mission's soup kitchen under pressure from his wife. Ron's wife dies of cancer, but he becomes friends with Denver Moore, a semi-literate homeless black man. As their friendship develops Denver asks:

I heard when white folks go fishin' they do somethin' called "catch and release." That really bothers me, I just can't figure it out. When colored folks go fishin', we really proud of what we catch, and we take it and show it off and we eat the catch, so it bothers me white folks would go to all the trouble to catch a fish, then when they done caught it, just throw it back in the water...So, Mr. Ron, it occurred to me: if you is fishin' for a friend you just gon' catch and releases, then I ain't got no desire to be your friend, but if you are lookin' for a real friend, then I'll be one. Forever.

The point is to be sincere in your volunteering and to be willing to take the risks and become involved in other people's lives. It is not fair to those you are helping to catch them and then release them. The list of opportunities is endless. Just ask, how can I help?

E. Family

The family part of the balance equation during retirement is completely different than when you were busy with your career. I remember the day I told my wife I needed to retire from oral and maxillofacial surgery because of my neurological disorder. She looked at me and said "What are you going to do now? You can't stay at home!" Her statement had a double meaning. First, she knew I would be miserable without a full agenda; second, I was now going to be invading her space. When you retire, you must honor your family's space, especially if you previously spent the majority of your time out of the house.

Many executives and professionals are accustomed to having multiple employees available to assist them in all sorts of endeavors. When you come home, it is not a good idea to give your spouse a list of what he or she needs to do for you, especially if he or she is still working full-time. I also do not advise rearranging your spouse's space, schedule, kitchen, or garage. There is nothing quite as annoying as a listless person rattling around the house; thus, finding a job or a volunteer position that excites you will be good for both you and your spouse.

Surviving the first few months of retirement will require some serious, straightforward communication. When a friend of mine retired, he was discussing with his wife the need to downsize their house. She looked at him and said, "Are we going to get rid of your junk or mine?" Although the exchange was humorous, these are real issues that couples must discuss.

The best piece of advice I can give you is to listen to your significant other. To do this, you have to give him or her your undivided attention, position yourself with open body posture, don't interrupt, and give him or her feedback. It goes without saying that couples must discuss everything from finances to the possibility of moving, but the most important aspect is finding out what your spouse needs to be happy during your retirement. This conversation may go differently than you'd think, but if your relationship was happy and successful before your retirement, then you should be successful with this next stage.

If you are single when you retire, I encourage you to develop a plan of how you want your extended family and friends to fit into your new life. If you are fortunate to have children and grandchildren, plan how you can be part of their lives without intruding. As a society, we have, for the most part, lost the art of staying connected with our families. Having time available to develop and redevelop relationships with children, grandchildren, and friends can be one of the most fulfilling aspects of retirement. The key here is that you are the one responsible for fostering the relationships; don't wait for your friends and family members to come to you. You cannot assume that because your days are open now, your friends and family members will show up on your front doorstep with lunch. They have busy lives, and you essentially have to ask permission to be more involved with them. Consider it like fishing—you throw out a hook and bait (by sending a few e-mails or making a few phone calls) and wait for a bite. If you end up contacting the same friend or family member three times in a row with no response, wait patiently. There may be a good explanation for that person's lack of response, or he or she may just not be interested. Testing the waters will take time and patience.

If you have become estranged from your family, consider apologizing for your absence in the past and make amends, even if you feel that the other person is the one in the wrong. Life is too short to hold grudges.

One of the greatest benefits of parenting and aging is seeing your children as adults. To do this you must take off the parent hat and become more of a friend. Ask your children or grandchildren their advice on life choices and what you plan to do in the future. One great way to reconnect with the younger generations is ask them to help you with technological advances, such as computers, smart phones, digital tablets, and so forth. Ask them to help you prepare your resume if you are going to re-enter the job market. Everyone likes to be asked for advice, but feel out your audience. I am fortunate to have three great son-in-laws, but it has been my experience that they really don't want my advice. However, by asking for theirs, we have reached a place of mutual respect. Work on your listening skills and be sincere in your approach.

Social networking may be a great catalyst in helping you reconnect with friends and family. By reaching out to someone on one of the popular social networking sites, you may open the door to a renewed relationship. One caveat is that people "connect" through social networking without any intention of forming real friendships. Just because an old friend accepts your "friend request" on Facebook does not mean that the relationship is sparked anew. Keep your expectations low and have patience.

F. Recreation

You may have once thought that you would devote your retirement to recreational activities, but you'll soon find that you need work, family, and spirituality as well to create balance. Just as we need to balance work, family, recreation, and spirituality, we need to balance our recreational activities. You should alternate between sedentary pursuits, such as reading, doing crossword puzzles or Sudoku, and playing bridge, with physical activity, such as golf, tennis, swimming, jogging, or skiing. Be sure to incorporate solo activities with social activities, and vary the people you do them with—go for a hike with your spouse, play catch in the yard with your grandchildren, see a movie with your children, and go to a wine tasting with friends. Study the language, food, and culture of a country with your family members and then visit that country—this is a great learning experience not only for you, but for any children in your family.

Make recreation a priority. Jot down some ideas and start making it happen. The physical, mental, and emotional rewards of recreation are critical to balance. I will expand on the benefits of physical and mental exercise in the chapter on aging.

G. Spirituality

Spirituality is different for everyone. It is a crucial part of maintaining a healthy and happy existence after you leave your day job. Spirituality doesn't necessarily require a religious affiliation; it is simply the practice of recognizing that you are part of something bigger than yourself. For some, spirituality comes in the form of hiking in the woods and appreciating nature. Others pray to God or practice meditation. Spirituality is whatever you make it.

I have relied on my personal faith in Christ and his teachings since a young child for comfort, assurance, and peace. It helps me to know that I am not going to be able go through life entirely by myself, and Christ keeps me company. I still hug the helm hard, trying to control everything and sometimes everyone around me, but my belief in Christ reminds me that I don't control much of anything, much less anybody.

Father James Martin, a Jesuit priest, summed up his view of religion when he wrote in *Between Heaven and Mirth: Why Joy, Humor and Laughter are at the Heart of the Spiritual Life* (Harper One, 2011), "False religion is the idea that if you believe, all will go well, and there is nothing to worry about. Real religion is the idea that if you believe, all may not go well, but, in the end, there is nothing to worry about." This thought may help carry you as you begin on your journey toward a successful and fulfilling retirement—not everything will go well, but in the end, everything will be okay.

If you are affiliated with a religion, continue practicing and worshiping, or if you have let your spirituality lapse over the years, rediscover your faith or connection to the greater universe. Experiment, explore, and find what is comfortable for you.

In addition to peace of mind and comfort, spirituality can offer some social and health benefits. Religious congregations often serve as social circles to provide mutual support for the young and the old, the rich and the poor, and everyone in between. A 1979 *Journal of Epidemiology* study revolutionized our understanding of the affect the social environment has on health. The nine-year study involved nearly 7,000 adults. The researchers studied social ties, including family relationships, friendships, and community groups, and membership in a church or a temple. The researchers found that the most socially isolated people with the fewest ties to others were at the highest risk of mortality, even when they adjusted for the health status of the respondents at the beginning of the study and certain risky behaviors, such as smoking, obesity, lack of physical activity, and lack of health services[2]. A 1988 study in *Science*, "Social relationships and health," confirms the importance of social ties in general, including membership or attendance at religious services[3].

If you are not already affiliated with a house of worship, you may need to attend services at several churches, temples, or mosques to find the right fit. And given the evidence supporting social ties and health, even if you don't derive much inspiration from a sermon or service, go for the coffee, cookies, and conversations.

Allan Hamilton, MD, a Harvard-educated neurosurgeon, wrote *The Scalpel and the Soul: Encounters with Surgery, the Supernatural, and the Healing Power of Hope* (Penguin, 2008). He enumerates stories of faith, healing, and the mysteries of the supernatural in his practice of neurosurgery and his journey through life. It is an

---

[2] Berkman L and Syme L. "Social Networks, Host Resistance, and Mortality, a Nine-Year Follow-Up Study of Alameda County Residents," *American Journal of Epidemiology*. 109(2): 186-204.
[3] House JS, Landis KR, Umberson D. "Social Relationships and Health," *Science*. 241(4865): 540-545.

insightful read. His appendix is well worth noting and, in my opinion, should be laminated and put on your mirror. He introduces his "Twenty Rules to Live By" by stating, "We cannot be ordered to love God. As powerful as God may be, no authentic love could exist between a human being and God without the freedom to choose. God's love may be boundless and everlasting, but each one of us alone must decide whether to declare it mutual."

One important aspect of spirituality is prayer. Regardless of whether you choose to affiliate yourself with a house of worship or attend services, you may fulfill your spiritual needs through solo prayer. Mitchell Krucoff, MD, a professor of medicine and cardiology at Duke University Medical Center, states that prayer "is the most ancient, widely practiced therapy on the face of the earth."

To maintain balance, I suggest that everyone carve out a bit of their day or week to consider God or an entity greater than oneself. This may take the form of prayer, meditation, yoga, or being alone to contemplate life. You may read religious texts or other sources that can give you peace and comfort in a troubled world. Taking time to contemplate your place in the world will lower your blood pressure, help your relationships, help you sleep better, and probably help you to be a better spouse, father, mother, friend, or child. Robert Fulgham, a popular author of *All I Really Need to Know I Learned in Kindergarten* and other books, says, "Be aware of wonder. Live a balanced life—learn some and think some and draw and paint and sing and dance and play and work every day some."

H. Lou's Story: Finding Balance

For Lou Hendrickx, balance didn't come until he retired from his position as a division chief for the Central Intelligence Agency in Virginia. In his job, he carried a beeper 24/7 to handle issues for 2,500 employees worldwide. Earlier in his career, he served in the Situation Room of the Johnson and Nixon administrations. After such an intense career, retirement was not easy.

When Lou retired, he started volunteering for Court Appointed Special Advocate for Children (CASA). A CASA volunteer is appointed by a juvenile judge and is required to meet with his or her appointed child, usually a physically or sexually abused child, every six months to ensure that the child has the proper foster, medical, and psychological care, and that his or her educational needs are properly met.

Although not required as part of the program, Lou worked with young men between the ages of 12 and 16, teaching them to play golf, drive his truck, hike, and appreciate the outdoors. These activities were a great opportunity to reinforce integrity, patience, and the value of life itself. He served as the mentor they never had.

Lou wrote poetry, went on archaeology digs, and hiked rim-to-rim in the Grand Canyon, Big Bend, the United States and Canadian Rockies, and the North and South Islands of New Zealand. He continued to play golf for the fellowship and exercise. He satisfies his spiritual needs by spending time in and with nature.

He remarried and reconnected with his brother, sister, nephews, and nieces and has enlarged his own family with his wife's relatives. Family has become a large part of his full and happy life. At the age of 72, he states that he has not been bored a single day after retirement and life just gets better every day.

Chapter Three
SOLITUDE/BOREDOM

"All unhappiness of men arises from one single fact, that they cannot stay quietly in their own room...we require things to distract us from ourselves...hence it comes people so much love noise and stir...it comes that the pleasure of solitude is a thing incomprehensible."

Blaise Pascal, philosopher
and mathematician (1623-1662)

I used to have all of my free time scheduled weeks in advance. I absolutely hated being by myself. I would have rather starved than eat in a restaurant alone. It has taken me many years to finally be OK with solitude. My wife of 42 years is still my best friend and constant companion, but we both enjoy time by ourselves.

Whether you consider yourself an introvert or an extrovert, humans are social animals. We look forward to interacting with others. We enjoy the workplace, not only for the satisfaction of doing a job well, but for the acceptance and appreciation of our peers and those we serve. We enjoy our families and friends for similar reasons. We seek out team sports, hunting or fishing, and gardening clubs more for the fellowship than for the score, the fish, or the tomatoes.

Many of us will have periods of being alone secondary to a loss of a loved one or friend; therefore, it is a worthwhile pursuit to learn to be comfortable alone. As I explained in Chapter Two, there are many benefits to being part of a social group, and that should always be a goal of retirement, but there are times when just being alone is healthy and rewarding.

An article in the *Journal for the Theory of Social Behavior*, "Solitude: An Exploration of the Benefits of Being Alone" states, "The paradigm experience of solitude is a state characterized by disengagement from the immediate demands of other people, a state of reduced social inhibition, and increase freedom to select one's mental and physical activities."[4] It is this freedom that some people find overwhelming, while others find it re-energizing. Solitude has a good side and bad side, and we will explore both.

A. The Sunny Side of Solitude

Solitude can be explained as a state of seclusion or isolation. It can be voluntary or involuntary. Short-term solitude can be a positive endeavor. We need to disconnect, at times, not only from people, but also from our devices. Phones, computers, radio (especially talk radio), and printed media all keep us informed, connected, and energized, but it is a healthy respite to disconnect regularly. The freedom you experience when you shut off the chatter, when you are alone with your own thoughts, can result in creativity, self-assessment, self-awareness, and self-development. It can be a time for prayer and meditation, or you can spend that time simply reading a good book. It is a time to think about ourselves and our

---

[4] Long, Christopher, Averill James. *"Solitude: An Exploration of Benefits of Being Alone." Journal for the Theory of Social Behavior. 33:1, 21-44.*

priorities in novel ways. It is a time to think about what we have done and learn from it.

I learned the real meaning of solitude prior to my early retirement. I grew up in the city and knew nothing about cattle, bailing hay, soil samples, water wells, or anything else to do with ranching, but when I was in my early 50s; my wife and I bought a 200-acre ranch west of Fort Worth, which we named The Broken Jaw. The 100-year-old house on the property was still in good shape, and we inherited an old barn. I mended fences and worked the cattle (a crossbreed of Angus and Herefords called Black Baldies). We spent every weekend at the ranch for three years. I found real solitude sitting on a tractor plowing a field or just walking the property. It was such a diversion from my busy practice that I could not wait to get there every week for a few days.

I learned several lessons during our ranching days. The first is that a four-wheel vehicle just gets you stuck farther from the house. Second, burning brush allows you to meet all of your neighbors because they think you are going to burn up the whole county. Third, after I bought a very old hay bailer, I learned that I was not the smartest guy in the county (as I once thought).

The bailer needed a new belt soon after I bought it, so I took it in to have the belt replaced. The cost was going to be in excess of $700, which was not much less than I paid for the bailer. I went back to the old guy that sold me the bailer and asked him if I could just splice the belt. He said sure, gave me the stapling device and a piece of old belt that was in his storage shed and sent me on my way. The total cost was $7. I felt more accomplishment from repairing the bailer than spending hours repairing extensive facial fractures.

I was busy bailing one day when I smelled smoke. I looked around and saw that I had set about an acre of pasture on fire in a pretty stiff wind. We called the local volunteer fire department, which was too small to handle the fire, so they called the fire department from a nearby town. Between the two, they got the fire out in a little over an hour.

Now, before I tell the rest of this story, remember that I said I thought I was really smart. I decided I could figure out why the bailer started the fire. A couple of the tines that pick up the hay were hitting each other and causing a spark, so I removed them and started bailing again. Low and behold, the tines were not the cause, and I started yet another fire. I called the fire department again, and they put the fire out rather quickly this time. I will never forget the fire chief putting his arm on my shoulder and saying "Doc, you are not going to bail any more today, are you?"

I felt lower than a snake's belly, and I gave a rather large contribution to the volunteer fire department every year after that. I had to sell the ranch after my neck went south and I could not do the physical work it required, but it was a real treat to work the land and raise livestock from the hay we grew (I really appreciate a good steak now). But most of all, it was the solitude that I enjoyed. Instead of responding to beepers, patients, and physicians, like I did during the week, I only answered to the land (and the fire department) on my weekends.

I don't share my story to suggest that you can't achieve solitude unless you buy a weekend property. Find solitude in your daily life by going for walks, getting up early before the rest of the family stirs, or taking a solo day trip to a national park. There are plenty of ways to cut out the chatter and be alone with your thoughts for a while.

Solitude becomes a great time for creativity. No one appreciated solitude better than American author Henry David Thoreau. He wrote in *Walden*, "I went to the woods because I wished to live deliberately, to front only the essential facts of life, and see if I could not learn what it had to teach, and not, when I came to die, discover that I had not lived." My favorite Thoreau quote is, "Many men go fishing all their lives without knowing that it is not fish they are after."

B. Leave your legacy

Use your solitude to paint, draw, and create with your hands or your head. I would encourage everyone to write their own life story—not necessarily for publication, but for family and friends. It sounds morbid, but everyone wants to be remembered and to influence others even after death, and spending your solitude creating this legacy can be fulfilling.

David Brooks, an editorial writer for *The New York Times* wrote about what he called a "life report." He suggests that everyone write a brief essay divided into life categories (career, family, faith, community, and self-knowledge) and give him- or herself a grade in each area. This is a great exercise to help you step back and take a look at your own life through your own eyes. However, the real benefit may be to our children and grandchildren. As Brooks states:

Young people are educated in many ways, but they are given relatively little help in understanding how a life develops, how careers and families evolve, what are the common mistakes and the common blessings of modern adulthood. The essays will help them benefit from your experience.

I had a good friend, Gary Reeves, PhD, that I spent many hours with hunting, playing golf, and just discussing matters of importance to us. He died suddenly before I could interview him for this book. During the two years prior to his death, he wrote a biography for his three children and grandchildren so they would understand what made him who he was. He sent me a copy to review, and it was both interesting and revealing. In some ways, I did not really know my friend. Gary's second book was *How the Bible Fits Together*, which he wrote as a result of self-study. Neither book was published, but that was not the point. Both books served the purpose of helping his friends and family better understand the man he was.

If writing is not your thing, you may enjoy spending your solitude creating art. I have another friend, Robert Karper, MD, a retired pathologist, who spends his solitude, as he describes it, "making sawdust." He is a master woodworker. He has made multiple pieces of exquisite furniture, bird feeders, bowls, and rolling pins for his family and friends. He is not a writer, but all his family members and friends have something to remember him by that was important to him. What a gift!

C. The Dark Side of Solitude

Solitude isn't always peaceful. For some people, too much solitude can lead to boredom and/or depression. For me (and I suspect for most of us), solitude is a short-term endeavor, but prolonged, it can be a prison sentence. I love people. I am ashamed to say that I still get bored at times. I had such a hectic, driven, goal-oriented life and career from the time I was 17 until I had to retire at the age of 55, that I never had time to even consider being bored. But an interesting lesson I learned from my friend Vern Oechsle is that "bored" is just another word for "lazy." His advice is to get off your butt.

I hate being bored, but more than that, my wife hates it when I say, "I am bored." Boredom could be interpreted as a lack of excitement or not wanting to accept life as it is. It may be the unwillingness to accept who we are, where we are, and what we are. Retirement, or the thought of retirement, can bring boredom to the forefront for many boomers.

Boredom can be considered a form of worry. It assumes that the rest of the world is out there having fun and you're stuck at home with nothing to do. It's a selfish and self-defeating feeling, as many of us will feel sorry for ourselves, be unappreciative of our many opportunities, and wait for someone or something to get us out of our boredom. It is not someone else's responsibility; staying engaged and productive is your responsibility. There is always an excuse not to engage in an activity—you'd like to paint but don't feel that you are good at it, you'd like to volunteer at the soup kitchen but don't feel that you're a people person, you'd like to take a trip to another country but are overwhelmed by the research involved. These are merely excuses hiding fear—fear of failure, fear of trying something new, fear of being alone. Whatever it is, take the first step to overcome it before you end up rattling around the house feeling lonely and bored month after month.

Most of us can leave the house, change activities, meet new people, and learn new information or skills, but we still sit around feeling bored. That is because anything done often enough can become boring; no matter how exciting it was to start. Your day can be busy from dawn until dusk, but if the activities aren't interesting to you, then boredom is inevitable. This book is about not ever being bored; rather, I hope it is a springboard to help you keep changing, learning, and helping others. Boredom can be trivial or it can be all-consuming and lead to psychological, physical, and social problems.

The distinction between boredom and depression is that boredom is a lack of interesting things to do, as opposed to depression, which is not having an interest in doing things. Boredom is temporary; depression may not be. Boredom should be easily resolved (get off your rear and go do something); depression is not something you can always resolve by yourself. In other words, there is not really an excuse for being bored, but there are reasons out of your control for being depressed. Both need to be addressed.

It is beyond the scope of this book to discuss depression and all of its ramifications, but it is imperative to at least understand the basics. A life change as significant as retirement can trigger bouts of depression. Some one-on-

one or group therapy can do wonders, and if needed, a little medication can give you the boost you need to tackle the problem head-on. Do not be ashamed if you think you might be suffering from depression—it is an extremely treatable condition, and once it's under wraps, you will have the freedom and motivation to enjoy your retirement.

All of us have periods of depression in life. We feel sad, lonely, unappreciated, and irrelevant at times. Feeling depressed is a normal physiologic and psychological reaction to loss, whether it is a loved one or a job or profession we have enjoyed. The risk of suffering a major depressive episode at some point during our lives is 12% for men and 25% for women[5]. When the feelings persist, there may be a problem worth seeking professional help. The National Institute of Mental Health lists the symptoms of depression as:

- Difficulty concentrating, remembering details, or making decisions

_____

[5] www.depressionstatistics.org

- Fatigue and decreased energy
- Feelings of guilt, worthlessness, and helplessness
- Insomnia, early morning wakefulness, or excessive sleeping
- Irritability and restlessness
- Loss of interest in activities or hobbies that were once pleasurable, including sex
- Overeating or appetite loss, headaches, aches and pains, or prolonged digestive symptoms
- Thoughts of suicide or suicide attempts

You do not have to experience every symptom in this laundry list to be depressed; usually five of them warrant a diagnosis. Again all of us experience the feelings on this list from time to time, except for the thoughts of suicide. Experiencing a few of these feelings does not mean you are abnormal, just human.

Mental health professionals characterize depression into five basic categories:

- Major depression
- Dysthymia (low-grade depression)

- Atypical depression
- Seasonal affective disorder
- Bipolar disorder

Individuals with a history of major depression or bipolar depression may have been diagnosed and treated earlier in life, but dysthymia and atypical depression can be subtle and difficult to recognize; thus, individuals with dysthymia or atypical depression may go undiagnosed for years. Anyone can develop depression, but the major risk factors are being female, having a parent or sibling with depression, lacking social supports, experiencing a significant alteration or stressful life events, or having a current alcohol or substance abuse problem.

As an aside, alcohol abuse among physicians is not related to medical specialty, type of practice, citizenship, or religion, but it is related to gender and age (males tend to drink more and more often than females)[6]. Heavy

---

6 WE McAuliffe, M Rohman, et al. Alcohol use and abuse in random samples of physicians and medical students. American Journal of Public Health. 81: 177-182. 1991.

drinking decreases with age in the general population but increases in older physicians. Now that is a scary finding.

The causes of depression are not completely understood. Studies suggest that depression results from an imbalance of neurochemicals, which include serotonin, norepinephrine, and dopamine. Stress also appears to play a major role in that it affects glucocorticoid release by the adrenal glands, which may result in a hyperactive relationship between the glucocorticoids and the hypothalamus in the brain. Glucocorticoids regulate the metabolism and immune system. Depression is probably caused by the interaction of these chemicals, as well as some environmental factors, such as major life changes, the death of a close friend or relative, or lack of stimulation. Mental illness is not just "being crazy." There is often a disruption in the chemical neurotransmitters, and medication and therapy can help.

The point of all of this scientific jargon is that sometimes you just can't "snap out of it." You may need specific medications designed to alter the aforementioned levels of neurochemicals.

I hope that this discussion of depression will motivate those of you who feel a loss by having to retire to evaluate and appreciate your feelings. Please don't hesitate to ask your physician for help if the sad feelings persist. The help is painless, inexpensive, and successful.

When it comes to thinking that the statistics don't apply to them, physicians are the worst offenders. But it's not just physicians—many executives have spent a lifetime sitting behind a desk and making excuses for not exercising or not eating well. If you're reading this book, most likely your career trumped healthy habits in the past, so I hope this chapter inspires healthy changes during your retirement.

A. The Science Behind Exercise, Diet, and Sleep for the Chronologically Impaired

You may have thought that you were bullet proof until you hit your late 50s or early 60s, at which point all kinds of things started to happen. Perhaps you developed a spare tire around the waistline, get winded going up a flight of stairs, or have stern orders from your physician to lay off the wine and cheese. If you are going to enjoy our retirement, you have to either adopt a healthy lifestyle (assuming you don't have one already) or maintain the healthy habits you currently practice. Almost everything in this book depends on being able to physically and mentally participate. I did not embrace a healthy lifestyle until the age of 62, which is really too late to start paying attention to good health. It is what you learn after you know it all that really counts, I suppose.

As you probably suspect, all kinds of bad things happen as we age. The heart's capacity to pump oxygenated blood starts decreasing after the age of 30. A healthy 25-year-old heart pumps 2 1/2 quarts of blood every minute, whereas a 65-year-old heart pumps 1 1/2 quarts a minute. This results in fatigue and breathlessness in modest daily activities[7]. Women, on the other hand, have an earlier drop in cardiac output, but then it appears to stabilize, while men have a progressive drop in the same function as they age[8].

Most Americans put on three to four pounds a year starting in midlife. Men start to lose muscle in their 40s, and the loss of muscle eventually reduces a man's

---

[7] *Harvard Men's Health Watch*, Dec., 2005.

[8] Knighten, V, Luisada, AA, Bhat, PK. "Changes in Cardiac Output Caused by Aging," *Angiology*, Feb., 1980, Vol. 31, 75-81.

musculature to 50% of what it was during the younger years. That extra weight is fat[9]. The added fat contributes to a rise in low-density lipoprotein (LDL, or "bad cholesterol") and a fall in high-density lipoprotein (HDL, or "good cholesterol"). Men and premenopausal women process cholesterol differently. Young women tend to have lower LDL levels than young men, and from puberty on, women tend to have higher levels of HDL than men. When estrogen production declines after menopause, a woman's HDL levels decrease greatly. After the age of 55, women tend to have higher levels of bad cholesterol than men[10]. If gaining three to four pounds a year wasn't bad enough, blood sugar levels rise about six points per decade, making type 2 diabetes distressingly common in senior citizens. Diabetes is related more to obesity than gender.

The good news is that exercise can help prevent the added pounds and subsequent ill-effects. You can reap

---

[9] *Harvard Men's Health Watch*, Dec., 2005.
[10] Robb, Barbara. "High Cholesterol: Why Your Gender Matters." *www.everdayhealth.com*. Dec., 2011.

the benefits through 30 to 60 minutes of continuous exercise three days per week. Researchers estimate that a 30% to 40% reduction in cardiovascular events is possible if most Americans met the government's recommendations for activity[11].

As we age, calcium levels drop, making both men and women more prone to osteoporosis and fractures (osteoporosis is more common and severe in women). Cognitive changes begin as early as age 45 (more on this later). Reflexes slow, and reaction times increase. Our hearing worsens, our vision starts failing, and many older folks develop obstructive sleep apnea. Does this scare you? Good. The truth is that none of this can be stopped entirely, but it can be slowed through a healthy diet and plenty of exercise.

Robert Karper, MD, a board certified physician in anatomical and clinical pathology and hematology/pathology, is a friend of mine who was

---

[11] Meyers, Jonathan. "Exercise and Cardiovascular Health" Circulation, 2003, e2-e5.

generous enough to share his thoughts on diet and exercise. He writes:

In some ways, I could compare lifestyle to a marathon race. You're not attempting to win, only to finish within your goals and abilities. One major obstacle in running a marathon is hitting the "wall." The wall comes when your muscles run out of glycogen. From that point on, your body doesn't respond to commands, and every movement requires great willpower. The race is no longer fun. Just finishing becomes problematic. The goal of training is to push that wall out as far as possible.

We are all going to die no matter what we do. Some of my friends see old people who are in ill-health, struggling just to meet their daily needs and taking a bucket full of very expensive pills. My friends put those two together and conclude, "I'm going to eat, drink, and be merry, and so what if I miss those last years of ill-health?" Their vision is that they will live happily, and in their mid-60s, they will clutch their chests and collapse with smiles on their faces. They might. They might even live to an advanced age if their genetics are great and God is willing. However, a more probable scenario is they will "hit the wall" in their early 50s. From that point on, they will struggle with obesity, arthritis, diabetes, failing kidneys, failing eyesight, neuropathy, peripheral artery disease, amputations, heart disease, and strokes, to name a few. Like a marathon, life is really not fun after you hit the wall, and all of the health problems could have been prevented had they adopted healthy lifestyles 30 years before. Jack LaLanne, in my view, represents one of the elite of life's marathon runners. By all accounts, he exercised daily, ate healthy, and managed to push the wall beyond his life span. He exercised and enjoyed excellent health until he suddenly died of pneumonia at age 96 (maybe because he refused to see a doctor).

B. Holding Off the Grim Reaper with Exercise

I hate exercise, always have. I played competitive tennis for 40 years, and then progressed to walking while playing golf. Now at 65, I ride in a golf cart with everyone else and have an occasional cigar. I was blessed with good genes; my dad died at 95 after a brief illness, and my mom is 93 and is still going strong. I am 6 feet 2 inches tall and weigh 190 pounds, on a good day. I thought I would always be the Teflon man and weight would not stick to me, but I was wrong.

As I got older, I starting noticing that swinging the grandkids around hurt by back and my shoulder, so I reluctantly began an exercise program at a local gym. I hired a trainer who is an ex-convict and a minister (there was no way that I was not going to do what he said). He designed an exercise regimen to strengthen my core, improve my golf game, and allow me to swing my grandkids around without injuring myself. Having an appointed time to meet him and having to pay him whether I showed up or not kept me motivated. It has been three years now and I am still going to the gym two or three times a week.

After a year, I began exercising without the trainer, doing resistance training with weight machines and cardio on a treadmill or stationary bicycle. I feel better, my golf game has improved, and I don't hurt myself playing with the grandkids. As we discuss aging and health during retirement, exercise will be a large part of maintaining, or in some cases, attaining good health.

Exercise makes you feel better. Usually, you can benefit from a mood boost within five minutes after moderate exercise[12]. In fact, research has shown that physical activity can not only help alleviate short-term depression, but it can relieve and even prevent long-term depression[13]. The mechanisms are not completely clear, but it is thought that exercise increases serotonin levels, which normalize sleep, and sleep helps protect the brain[14]. Exercise may also help slow mild to moderate dementia. A *Journal of the American Geriatric Society* study found that an exercise regimen of one hour twice a

---

[12] American Psychological Association's *Monitor on Psychology,* Dec. 2011. *www.apa.org/monitor/2011/12/exercise.aspx*

[13] Barbour KA, Edenfield TM, Blumenthal JA. "Exercise as a treatment for depression and other psychiatric disorders: a review." *J Cardiopulm Rehabil Prev.* 2007 Nov-Dec;27 (6):359-67.

[14] *Psychosomatic Medicine,* 2007, 2010

week resulted in significantly lower cognitive decline in patients in a retirement center[15].

Dr. William Buchan, an 18th century Scottish physician, wrote "Of all the causes which conspire to render the life of man short and miserable, none have greater influence than the want of proper exercise." He has a good point. Endurance training is the best exercise to improve cardiovascular function and can slow down the ill effects of aging. The key is to do movement-oriented activities regularly. The activities can be as simple as walking briskly 30 minutes a day, but can be as vigorous as jogging, rowing, swimming, cycling, cross country skiing, or even golf if you walk the course.

Your activity should result in a faster prolonged heart rate for at least 30 minutes a day. But you can't just walk around the block and call it a day. Add to your cardiovascular exercise some resistance training with machines or light weights, which will add muscle mass

---

[15] Rolland Y, et al, "Exercise program for nursing home residents with Alzheimer's disease." *J Am Geriatr Soc* 55. 148-165, 2007.

and preserve bone calcium. Resistance training prevents sarcopenia and osteoporosis, which don't sound as lethal as they really are. Karper says that together, sarcopenia and osteoporosis contribute to falls, which are a major cause of morbidity in the elderly. The immediate mortality of a hip fracture is around 10% and climbs to greater than 30% after a year. Those who survive are left to deal with loss of mobility and risk of infection. Strength training can help prevent osteoarthritis (wear and tear arthritis), as well, by strengthening the muscles and ligaments, thereby stabilizing the joint. Paradoxically, if you already have the beginnings of arthritis, resting will make it worse.

High repetitions (15 to 20 reps to exhaust the muscle) with a lighter weight build strength and endurance. Fewer repetitions (8 to 10) with a heavier weight build bulk. Karper recommends starting with a weight and an exercise of which you can easily perform 20 reps. After several weeks, add weight until you can barely get 10 to 12 reps before exhaustion and work your way back up to 20. You need at least two days to let your muscles recover from a heavy workout, but you can alternate muscle groups if you work out more often. For example, you can exercise your upper body on Mondays and Thursdays and your lower body on Tuesdays and Fridays.

Flexibility training and balance exercises round out the routine and can include yoga or Tai Chi. Karper says that he never stretched before his mid-50s. His trainers explained that exercising without stretching is like driving with the brake on: you can't move efficiently and it's hard on the parts. Balance work is also important. Karper's favorite balance exercise is to stand on a Bosu ball and have someone throw a medicine ball toward you. Catching the ball while maintaining your balance on the soft surface can strengthen your core and improve balance.

Dedicate 20 minutes each to cardiovascular fitness, strength training, and stretching, and you'll be done in one hour. When it comes to your body, if you do not use it, you will lose it.

Karper shares his experience with exercise throughout the aging process:

Life was too busy for me to be Jack LaLanne. In my early life, I concentrated on cardiovascular fitness. I ran, bicycled, and climbed mountains. As I have aged, I have added strength training to my efforts. I ran around the neighborhood and met lots of other runners. We are still great friends and had many great conversations while we ran. It was fun, but it also smoothed out the rest of my life. Stress didn't bother me as much even though I worked in a stressful world. I slept like a baby, ate like a horse, and had no physical limitations.

You don't have to run a marathon to be fit. You just need to do something for 20 minutes, three times a week, at minimum. That something should get your heart rate up to 60-80% of your maximum (220 minus your age multiplied by 0.8). To help fill in the gaps that reality creates, I also try to incorporate exercise into daily life. I don't circle for 15 minutes trying to find a close parking space. I intentionally find the easy one farthest from the door. I take the stairs (although I must admit, if it's more than six floors, I take the elevator. Otherwise, you smell bad when you get there). Everyone can think of something for their break time besides sitting down to the feed bag. Start a walking group, it's more fun.

C. Stop Eating Pimento Loaf and Twinkies

You probably don't want to hear it again, but everyone should reduce his or her intake of saturated fats, trans fats, and sources of cholesterol. Trans fats came into the spotlight a few years ago and quickly earn a bad reputation for lowering HDL cholesterol and raising LDL, thus increasing the risk of coronary heart disease.

Cholesterol is a waxy substance that is a major component of the plaque that obstructs blood flow, causing arteriosclerosis. When an artery is narrowed enough that the organ involved doesn't get enough blood to live, you have a heart attack, stroke, or lose a foot to amputation. Surprisingly, the cholesterol you eat is irrelevant within reason. You can ignore marketing statements like "a cholesterol-free food." Fat is the problem. For reasons that are not clearly understood, the type of fat you eat has the largest effect on cholesterol.

Fat is a long-chain molecule that has a carbon backbone and hydrogen atoms on the sides. If some hydrogen molecules are missing, it is unsaturated. Monounsaturated fats have one pair of hydrogen molecules missing and polyunsaturated fats have more than one hydrogen molecule missing. Saturated fat has all of its hydrogen molecules. Saturated fats are straight and easily line up with one another to form a solid at room temperature. Unsaturated fats have a bend, don't line up as well, and are liquid at room temperature. This feature makes it easy to tell the good fat from bad. Saturated fats are solid at room temperature (butter, lard), raise bad cholesterol, and may lower good cholesterol. Monounsaturated fats (olive oil) lower bad cholesterol and raise good cholesterol. They are liquid at room temperature. Polyunsaturated fats (canola oil, corn oil) are also liquid and lower bad cholesterol but don't change HDL. Plants tend to contain unsaturated fats, and animals contain saturated fats.

Add foods to your diet that have omega 3 fatty acids and monounsaturated fats, which are found in fish, sardines, nuts, olive oil, and avocados. Eat lots of fruits and vegetables (especially broccoli), whole grains, and low- or non-fat dairy products. Decrease your sugar intake, and try to get 15% of your calories from protein.

Throw away the salt shaker; sodium can raise blood pressure. The lower your blood pressure and cholesterol, the better. As far as blood pressure is concerned, when it is even just a little high, it pounds your arteries, and salt is the main culprit. Some people can eat salt to their heart's content (no pun intended) and never get hypertension. Others get it regardless of what they do. There is a large group of people who are prone to hypertension, and if you are one of them, don't eat much salt (1500 to 2300 milligrams per day). Look for hidden salt in restaurants and prepared supermarket foods. Even if you request a low-salt meal at a restaurant, most sauces are premade, and the meat is brined.

Unsaturated fats tend to turn rancid quickly because the unsaturated part reacts with air. Manufacturers have understood this for a long time, but there is only so much lard available, so they artificially add hydrogen to more abundant plant oils. This process creates trans fats, which are the worst of them all and should be avoided at all costs. If you see "partially hydrogenated oil" on the label, don't eat it. Hard-stick margarine and shortening are much worse than butter and lard (which aren't good) but can still be labeled "all vegetable and cholesterol-free."

Alcohol should be limited to two glasses of wine a day for males, and one glass for females. It is unfair, but alcohol is thought protect the heart in both men and women in moderate amounts, but more than one glass a day for women may increase the risk of breast cancer. Of course tobacco in any form is not helpful to either the smoker, or those subjected to the second-hand smoke. Although coffee was under scrutiny for a while, it is now thought to be beneficial in moderation. I was encouraged when nutritionists finally said dark chocolate[16] and nuts are good for you, but I am just waiting for the day they say I can have it over ice cream.

---

[16] "Is Chocolate Good for Your Heart?" Cleveland Clinic, Jan. 2012. *http://my.clevelandclinic.org/heart/prevention/nutrition/chocolate.aspx*

As you've probably heard numerous times by now, diets don't work. Losing weight is something that is achieved through permanent lifestyle changes. Karper writes:

There are a few lucky individuals who are thin genetically. The rest of us crave calories and must fight weight gain forever. Sorry, it's not a temporary diet but a way of life. The only thing that ultimately matters is calories in versus calories out. If you eat more calories than you expend, you will gain weight. It is shocking how tightly controlled calories must be to maintain weight. Eating just one extra teaspoon of sugar a day will cause over a one pound weight gain in a year. I weighed 160 pounds in medical school and now weigh 195 pounds (first thing in the morning with my teeth brushed, an empty bladder, and fingernails clipped). I'd like to think it is because I've been lifting weights, but more likely, it is that teaspoon of sugar. I typically gain two to three pounds each fall and lose one to two pounds each spring. Over 35 years, with one pound per year, I got to 195 pounds. I recommend learning to read food labels, paying attention to calories, weighing in every morning, and if all else fails, get an app for your phone that keeps track of your calories for you. I also recommend working on both sides of the equation – exercise and diet. If you only diet, your body knows fat is missing and thinks there is a famine. It shuts down your metabolism (meaning you require even fewer calories per day) and your fat cells will do everything they can to get it back. Statistically, diets don't work and you gain back the weight as soon as you quit.

According to the World Health Organization, 10 out of 15 causes of death in adults aged 60 years or older are ischemic heart disease, cerebrovascular disease, diabetes, hypertension, stomach cancers, colon/rectal cancers, nephritis, renal disease, liver cancer, cirrhosis of the liver, and breast cancer. Arguably, all are influenced by dietary intake, smoking, and physical activity. There's a reality check for you.

D. Get Your Beauty Sleep

Sleep has always been a priority for me, and I am blessed with the ability to fall asleep quickly and sleep soundly the entire night. My friends say I can do this because I have no conscience. For many others, sleep is a struggle despite how critical it is to good health and longevity. Sleep is when our body reboots; some functions slow down, some increase when we sleep. Serotonin, which we discussed in the chapter on solitude, actually decreases while we sleep, but it is required for the production of melatonin, which helps us sleep[17]. Sleep helps us handle pain and stress, concentrate better, and basically make us more agreeable and sociable. People who are sleep deprived can be real grouches.

Factors that can lead to poor quality sleep are being awakened during the night by external factors (loud neighbors, a room that is too hot or too cold, a TV that no one shut off), smoking and drinking alcohol late in the evening (use alcohol as a drink, not a drug), as well as overeating and resulting symptoms of acid reflux.

The stress of retirement, the change in routines, and fear of the unknown will, at least for a time, lead to sleepless nights and waking up at two o'clock in the morning with a

---

[17] Hart, Carol. *Secrets of Serotonin: The Natural Hormone that Curbs Food Cravings, Reduces Pain, and Elevates Your Mood.* St. Martin's Griffin, 2008.

list of stuff you think you need to do. Many of the people I interviewed also admitted to having dreams of their work experience, which can be good or bad, but disruptive nonetheless. The Mayo Clinic recommends seven sleep tips[18]:

- Go the bed at the same time every night
- Don't go to bed hungry or stuffed and avoid caffeine and nicotine before bed
- Create a bed time ritual
- Get comfortable
- Limit your daytime naps
- Exercise during the day
- Manage your stress

If you are prone to making lists, keep paper and a pen at your bedside so you can jot down your list and forget about it instead of keeping yourself up worrying about it.

---

[18] Mayo Clinic. "Sleep Tips: 7 Steps to Better Sleep." www.mayoclinic. com/health/sleep/HQO1387. July, 2011.

Older people do appear to need less sleep than younger people[19]. Younger people get nine hours of sleep, whereas older people tend to get about seven and a half hours. If you are not obtaining the minimum amount of sleep, talk to your doctor about being evaluated through a sleep study. You may find that your insomnia is caused by reasons you are not aware of.

E. Where Did I Put My Keys?

As we age, the most noticeable changes are often the physical ones. But changes occur within our brains as well. We start to forget things, we don't react as quickly as we used to, and our car keys keep disappearing. One of the major concerns for older folks is the possibility of developing dementia. There are several forms of dementia or cognitive decline; some are a normal part of aging and some are not.

---

19 Dijk, Derk-Jan and Klerman, Elizabeth. "Age-Related Reduction in the Maximal Capacity for Sleep—Implications for Insomnia." *Current Biology*. 18: 1118-1123. Aug. 2008.

The first sign of mild cognitive impairment is short-term memory loss. If you can't find your keys, that is normal; but if you can't find your car, you may have a problem. I have a friend in his 70s who keeps his keys in his BMW while it is on the street or in the parking lot. I asked him why he would do such a thing, and he responded, "It is easier to find my car than my keys." I asked him if his car ever gets stolen, and he said yes, the police always find it, and the windows are usually still intact. If you get to the point where it's easier to keep your keys in your car, it's time to speak to your physician about the possible development of a cognitive impairment.

The next stage is memory impairment during stressful situations, followed by a loss of executive function[20]. Executive function is one's ability to plan, make decisions, correct errors, trouble shoot, and navigate situations that require a course of action that has not been used before.

----

[20] Hirtz D, et al. "How common are the 'common' neurologic disorders?" *Neurology*, 68:326-37. 2007.

Most people can function pretty well, even with the loss of executive function; some are just better at hiding it than others. Usually, the person experiencing the cognitive decline is the last person to recognize the problem. As abnormal as it feels, short-term memory loss, memory impairment, and loss of executive function are all considered a normal part of aging.

In his early 90s, my dad developed a moderate cognitive impairment, but his personality and sense of humor remained intact. He and my mom were sitting out one evening looking at the lake where they lived, and my dad stated how lucky they were to have survived so long without having to take any medications. My mom reminded him that he took a memory pill and a sleeping pill every night. My dad responded, "Well, the memory pill isn't working."

The last two stages of cognitive decline before Alzheimer's is diagnosed are the ones that the medical community associates most often with dementia: depression, apathy, social withdrawal, geographical disorientation, and trouble finding words.

Some individuals will develop Alzheimer's disease, the granddaddy of cognitive impairments associated with aging. The prevalence of Alzheimer's disease doubles every five years after the age of 65. Fourteen percent of individuals 71 and older have some form of dementia, while 9.7% of the same patient population has Alzheimer's disease. At the age of 90, 37.4% have dementia, and 79.5% of these cases are Alzheimer's disease[21]. Alzheimer's disease is diagnosed through neuropsychological testing, magnetic resonance imaging scans, and positron emission tomography (PET) imaging studies. Mild cognitive impairment progresses to Alzheimer's disease about 4% of the time[22].

The risk factors for cognitive decline are similar to those for heart disease; some you can control and some you

---

[21] Plassman, et al. "Prevalence of Dementia in the United States: The Aging, Demographics, and Memory Study." *Neuroepidemeology* 29:125–132. 2007).

[22] Hirtz D, et al. "How common are the 'common' neurologic disorders?" *Neurology*, 68:326-37. 2007.

can't. The following is a list of risk factors associated with cognitive decline:

- Age
- Gender (women are more likely to become cognitively impaired than men)
- Family history of early onset dementia
- Depression
- Low levels of education
- High levels of C-reactive protein, seen in inflammation
- High levels of homocystine, seen in some heart disease
- Head trauma
- Tobacco, alcohol, or substance abuse
- Diabetes
- Fatty diet
- Untreated hypertension
- Obesity

Chronic alcohol abuse affects cognitive function and creates deficits in executive function, visuospatial abilities, and gait and balance. In some cases, the effects are permanent[23].

Amidst all of the disheartening statistics, there is some good news. The government and private enterprises are investing a great deal of money and effort to find a solution for Alzheimer's disease, dementia, and other cognitive impairments. It is a personal tragedy for the victims and their families, and it is a financial disaster to pay for their care.

There are a few activities that may help at least slow cognitive decline. Memory task training can increase short-term memory and general intelligence[24]. Doing crossword puzzles or Sudoku, playing solitaire, learning a language or musical instrument, or learning to dance can keep the brain active. Using the right side of the brain (the

---

[23] *Neuropsychiatry* study by EV Sullivan
[24] Sitzer DI, et al. "Cognitive Training in Alzheimer's Disease: A meta analysis of the Literature." *Acta Psychiatrica Scandinavica.* 114: 75-90. 2006.

creative side, as opposed to the logical side) appears to help slow the development of cognitive decline.

What is good for the heart is good for the head. Exercise and diet appear to help stave off cognitive decline. Statins, a class of drugs that cause the liver to absorb more cholesterol from the blood, appear to cut the risk of Alzheimer's in some patients with a predisposition. Vitamin B regimens decrease the levels of homocystine, and medications, such as Aricept, may slow down but do not prevent the decline. Vitamin E may protect the brain by attacking free radicals, and resveratrol, found in red wine, may protect brain cells from the formation of amyloids, proteins that lead to neurodegenerative disorders. It is the "sticky" stuff that messes up the wiring in the brains of Alzheimer's patients. Low-dose intravenous insulin appears to suppress the formation of amyloids as well[25].

---

[25] L Sanders, "Memories Can't Wait: Researchers Rethink the role of Amyloid in Causing Alzheimer's," *Science News*, March 12, 2011. P 22-28.

It is imperative to take an active part in attaining or maintaining your health in retirement, otherwise all that hard work you put in earlier in life will be for naught. Marcus Tullius Cicero summed it up when he said, "Advice in old age is foolish; for what can be more absurd than to increase our provisions for the road the nearer we approach our journey's end." Start now.

Chapter Five
MENTORSHIP/LEADERSHIP

"Mentoring is a brain to pick, an ear to listen, and a push in the right direction."

John C. Crosby,
American politician (1859-1943)

In this chapter, I hope to challenge you to take a risk in your retirement. It is not a risk to your financial wellbeing, or to what you accomplished in your pre-retirement life, but it may be risk to your time and possibly your ego. In Chapter Two, we discussed creating balance in your post-retirement life, and a mentoring relationship can fulfill part of the balance equation. Mentoring helps you to stay relevant in your retirement, but most of all, it puts you in a position to pay it forward. It is a way to share your leadership skills and life experience with others. If you were in a position of authority in your previous career, mentoring is the next step as you enter retirement. You have the ability to teach your leadership skills and confidence to someone else. Even if your career didn't offer a prestigious title or a boatload of responsibility, you have something to offer someone who is less fortunate or who is simply trying to better himself or herself.

A. Anyone Can Be a Mentor

The first step to being a mentor is to understand the role thoroughly. Mentoring relationships are often used in the business world to great advantage, but this discussion focuses on mentoring outside of the workplace.

Mentor was a Greek mythological figure to whom Odysseus entrusted the care of his son, Telemachus. Mentor was both a trusted counselor and teacher for Odysseus and his son. Today, the word mentor is used both as a noun and a verb; it is not to be confused with coaching. The two are different, and the difference is important.

Coaching is usually a part of mentoring, but most coaches are not mentors. The coaching relationship is limited to the particular task, job, or skill that you are attempting to teach, such as a golf swing, public speaking, fly fishing, or sewing. Mentoring is a relationship that should not be entered into without thought and conviction. Mentoring can be informal or formal, but it should always be voluntary and mutually agreeable between the mentor and the mentee. It is not sport fishing—the relationship does not end when the fish is caught. A mentor can be a facilitator, a coach, a listener, but most importantly, a friend who cares about his or her mentee's development. Mentoring is about finding life balance, discussing difficult choices, and sharing experiences, good and bad, with another person. Most of the time, an older person mentors a younger person, but this isn't always the case.

Being a mentor does not give you a title or a position of power or authority. It is servant leadership at its best. The role of mentor must be earned, it cannot be bestowed. It is teaching at its best, particularly in a Socratic form in which individuals engage in a debate to elicit ideas and further discussion. I have been blessed with several mentors in my life, and have also had the great privilege to be a mentor to others. It is a duty of the heart, not the mind. Mentoring can also be a reciprocal relationship where you learn from your mentee and he or she learns from you.

Mentoring can be as formal as joining Big Brothers Big Sisters (more on this later), or it can be as informal as spending a specific time each week with a grandchild. Informal mentoring does not require specific goals or metrics and, as a mentor, you can choose how much time and access you are going to give to your mentee. Formal mentoring, on the other hand, involves establishing goals; the mentor and mentee measure outcomes, and the mentor provides skill training and moral support to the mentee.

Mentors and mentees are paired based on compatibility and sometimes chemistry. In a formal relationship, mentorship is usually open to anyone who meets the standards and criteria of the organization that is coordinating the relationships. In informal relationships, you may stumble on your mentee serendipitously and feel that it is the right fit. Mentors, for purposes of this book, are not paid positions, but the non-monetary gains are significant.

B. Pay it Forward

There are many formal mentoring organizations available that pair adults with young people, but I will highlight Big Brothers Big Sisters because of its longevity and proven track record. Big Brothers started in 1904 when a young New York City court clerk named Ernest Coulter saw more and more young boys come through his court room. He set up an organization whereby caring adults could help many of these kids stay out of trouble. At about the same time, a group called Ladies of Charity were befriending girls who had come through New York's children's court system. This group eventually became known as Catholic Big Sisters. Both groups remained independent until 1977, when Big Brothers Association and the Big Sisters International joined to become Big Brothers Big Sisters of America. The Big Brothers Big Sisters website states "Each time we pair a child with a role model, we start something incredible: a one-to-one relationship built on trust and friendship that can blossom into a future of unlimited potential."

Big Brothers Big Sisters' statistics are remarkable. Public/Private Ventures, a national research organization, conducted an independent research project throughout 1994 and 1995. The organization studied two groups of children, 950 in total, with varying geographical and ethnic backgrounds, who joined the program. Half were randomly paired with a Big Brother or a Big Sister and half were placed on a waiting list. The researchers surveyed both the unmatched and matched children and their parents when they first applied and 18 months later. On average, a Big Brother or Big Sister met with an assigned child three times a month for one year. Compared to the children on the waiting list, the children who were matched to a mentor were 46% were less likely to begin using illegal drugs, 27% were less likely to begin using alcohol, 52% were less likely to skip school, 37% were less likely to skip a class, and 33% were less likely to hit someone. Public/Private Ventures also reported that the "littles" were more confident in their performance in school work and got along better with their families.

A pastor friend of mine, Hud McWilliams, who has a PhD in clinical psychology, said:

At the core of mankind is the need for secure attachment to others. The seeking of connection and the feelings that come with it—stability, safety, acceptance, nurturing, empathy, and respect—are at the center of any lasting relationship. Many of us lose the ability to form satisfying, enduring relationships as adults (much less as children) because of being stunted by destructive relational experiences, like abandonment, emotional deprivation, a message that we are personally defective, social exclusion, and rejection. Let's face it—good, robust, hardy, optimal relationships are hard to come by and are even harder to regain once the trust is damaged.

There are countless children in precarious environments, and one caring adult could make a huge and long-lasting difference in their lives.

C. Honesty, Trust, Positive Vision, and Emotional Intelligence

If you have decided to become a mentor, I encourage you to place yourself where you have something to offer. In Chapter Two, we discussed the various possibilities for finding the right fit—the same applies here. Identify what you excelled in at your previous job and figure out how it can be taught and modeled for your mentee. If you have a knack for explaining things to others, ask the local school about tutoring opportunities. If you have a strong business sense, take a budding entrepreneur under your wing. If you love being active, help a troubled teen stay off the streets by going for hikes, playing tennis, or taking a canoe trip together. If part of your previous job involved interviewing potential employees, help a struggling single mom in the community land a job that will help her get back on her feet.

D. Honesty and Trust

When you decide to become a mentor, the most important quality you can bring to the table is honesty. James Kouzes and Barry Posner, authors of The Truth About Leadership (Josey-Bass Press, 2010), have done extensive research on leadership over a 30-year period and have conducted more than 1 million surveys. The findings of their studies can just as easily apply to mentorship as they can to leadership. The number one attribute people look for in a leader is honesty. Honesty means different things to different people, but it is essentially doing the right thing when no one else is watching. It is playing golf by the rules, giving back incorrect change, and doing what you said you would do. It means telling the truth and having moral, ethical, and consistent standards applied equally to all people and in every circumstance. It means being honest with yourself, knowing your strengths, but more importantly knowing your weaknesses.

Kouzes and Posner also found that for leaders to be successful, they must be willing and able to trust those they are leading and simultaneously earn trust through actions, not words. Trust is important to all relationships, but it is essential to the mentoring relationship. Trust involves risks, and proving to others that you can be trusted takes time.

John Townsend, author of *Leadership Beyond Reason* (Thomas Nelson, 2009), makes a great observation:

I also observed that successful leaders have a high sense of responsibility over their lives. At the end of the day, they take accountability for their successes and failures. They have zero tolerance for blaming others and zero tolerance for excuses. They are harder on themselves than others.

Trust also comes from communicating clearly. Your mentee will interpret your statements, promises, and intentions in a way that makes the most sense for them. If a mentee has come from a troubled environment, he or she may interpret your statements and actions differently (i.e., defensively) than you intend. Therefore, it is up to you to communicate clearly. Ambiguity, evasiveness, and half-truths will not build trust. Body language, eye contact, and voice volume and cadence all play an important role in communication. You have to put yourself at your mentee's level both literally and figuratively. If you are speaking to a child, get down to their level. If you are speaking to an adult, sit together at a table (don't make the other person sit on the other side of an obtrusive desk). Sitting minimizes the height differential, which can affect the openness of a conversation.

E. Positive Vision

Kouzes and Posner found that successful leaders have a positive vision. Having a positive vision means not only being optimistic, but also looking forward, not to the past. No one wants to listen or learn from a negative person. Your mentee may have had a charmed life, but more likely than not, he or she will have been in an environment that is anything but positive or forward thinking. Forward thinking people are always learning, reading, researching, listening, and engaging others. Kouzes and Posner say it best:

Those who learn to be optimistic about life are far more likely to be successful than those who view the current events through the lens of a pessimist. This means that your outlook on the future or life in general strongly influences you and (those around you). In order to reach the top of the distant summit, you need to be optimistic, zestful, and energetic. You need to be curious about how things work and search for a deeper meaning and understanding of what's going on around you.

F. Emotional Intelligence

Emotional intelligence is critical to helping others to be productive and thoughtful citizens of the future. Daniel Goleman popularized the term "emotional intelligence" in 1998 when he published *Working with Emotional Intelligence* (Bantam Books, 2000). He builds the case that great leadership works through emotions, and thus is the key to a mentoring relationship. You have to not take yourself too seriously, meaning you have to be able to laugh at yourself and admit when you are wrong. Albert Einstein once stated, "We should take care not to make intellect our god. It has, of course, powerful muscles, but not personality. It cannot lead, only serve."

Self-awareness (i.e., being in sync with your own feelings) is the first step toward emotional intelligence. You should be realistic and constantly thoughtful and reflective. Self-management follows self-awareness. Challenge yourself to not speak impulsively, and when something bothers you, ask yourself why (be brutally honest when you answer yourself—you may be surprised by your answers). Keep your temper under control and try to be patient (my biggest challenge). When you're self-aware and practicing self-management, you cannot be held captive by your emotions.

The third piece of emotional intelligence, and maybe the most important attribute to have in a mentoring relationship, is social awareness. Once you are aware of how you feel and react around others, you become aware of how others feel and react around you. If you don't like it when people check their e-mail on their smartphones while you are trying to speak to them, chances are others don't like it either. Irish playwright George Bernard Shaw's play *Pygmalion* includes these poignant lines:

The secret Eliza is not having bad manners or good manners or any other particular sort of manners, but having the same manner for all human souls, in short, behaving as if you were in heaven, where there are no third class carriages. One soul is as good as another.

Put yourself in your mentee's shoes, and you'll probably find that they are too tight. If you are dogmatic and domineering, you will lose the relationship. If you are not aware of your mentee's financial, ethnic, and generational differences, you will not connect. To be effective, you have to see the world from their viewpoint. As you mentor, stay focused; listen and observe what your mentee is not only saying, but also feeling. Stop talking, stop thinking about what you are going to say next, and listen intently. Listening fully is not natural for most people, particularly if you have been in a position of power or influence. You can't listen to another person when your cell phone is ringing or when you are checking your e-mails or stock market reports. Turn the cellphone off, put the computer away, and commit to being silent.

Sincerity is the key to communication, and as a mentor, YOU are responsible for making communication happen. In her book *Overcoming Anger* (Adams Media, 2004), Carol Jones, PhD, describes empathetic listening:

If you can provide help by empathetic listening, so much the better. Remember, everyone is just trying to survive, doing the best they can, and you need to recognize their struggle. Empathy helps you avoid making judgments.

The point is to hear the whole story before making judgments.

I have always struggled with the concept that one or two really smart people always make the correct decisions. I am often wrong. Diversity and numbers always trump one or two smart guys. It is almost a given you will not be mentoring someone who looks like you or has had the same opportunities as you have. James Surowiecki, in *The Wisdom of Crowds* (Anchor Books, 2005), has the science to prove there is wisdom in crowds. Groups that include differing genders, ethnicity, and generations will nearly always come to a better conclusion than the two smart guys. The more diverse the group, the better they are at problem solving. In other words, be open-minded.

Although you may only be mentoring one person, the theory behind the wisdom of crowds still applies. Listen to your mentee's perspective and learn about his or her culture and generation. Despite your feelings otherwise, he or she may not be wrong. Each culture has its strengths, and each generation has something to offer. All generations value ethics and honesty and all want the same basic things: respect, trust, and the opportunity to learn and grow.

As evidenced by the personal stories throughout this book, baby boomers want to be asked to help and we enjoy public recognition of a job well done. Generation X does not like to be micro managed, and they enjoy seeing rapid progress toward their goals. Millennials (Generation Y) expect more coaching and mentoring, thrive with structure, and appreciate feedback. Of course, Generation X and Y are more technologically savvy and may be able to mentor you once you realize that your phone is smarter than you. Leverage the younger generations for their expertise; both of you will benefit.

The benefits of a mentoring relationship are endless, but you have to be there in the good times and bad. It is not a fair weather relationship. You have to be trusted and consistent and honest. Use what you learned in your other job to pay it forward to help the next generations.

G. Jim Rickman's Story: Mentoring the Next Generation

Jim Rickman is a civil engineer who retired at the age of 63. He spent 18 years in government service, planning, drafting, and checking soil and water conservation projects. His last few years in government service were dedicated to environmental engineering for the Department of Agriculture in the Southeast United States. He became a consultant in private industry, essentially doing the same thing for an additional seven years after he retired the first time. He found it satisfying to help reduce erosion and water pollution, and he loved the feeling that the work was improving the Earth.

Leadership was not something Jim understood or sought when he retired, but he has managed to share his leadership skills in the community as well as in a mentoring relationship. He was involved in the Jaycees, was trained as a leader, and became the president of the local chapter. He has been president of our local home owner's association (and the members would really like him to be president forever). In my opinion, he is a natural leader.

In addition to being a leader, Jim makes a great mentor. He enjoys spending time with his grandchildren, teaching them to think about how much better their lives will be if they develop a good work ethic and try to be useful. He uses the "bribe method" to encourage good grades, and he complements them when they work hard. He is passing down his personal values of honesty, truthfulness, and being respectful of others. His legacy is centered on knowing his children and grandchildren are kind and caring.

H. Jim Schierling's Story: Teaching Grace

Jim Schierling has a bachelor's degree in psychology, a master's in biblical exposition, and a doctorate of ministry in hermeneutics. He was the pastor of a Bible church for more than 30 years. He spent 70% of his time in pastoral counseling and 30% in sermon preparation. While pastoring, he was available six nights a week for meetings and counseling, and he protected one night a week for family time. It was a 24/7 on-call profession. Weddings, funerals, meetings, training, teaching, and mentoring filled the rest of his time. There was always a need. He spent a great deal of time conducting premarital counseling and had couples sign a contract agreeing that if they ever considered divorce, they would come see him before consulting an attorney. He enjoyed the fact that he was "equipping people for maturity in this life that makes an investment for eternity."

When Jim retired at the age of 63, seven years ago, which is unusual for pastors, he was available to his wife and grandchildren. He had only been home in the evening on Monday nights for his entire career. Suddenly, balance became a possibility. His wife was a retired teacher, and they coordinated their calendars so they could enjoy their freedom and priorities. They finally were able to eat together in the evenings. His primary purpose in retirement has been to mentor other pastors and his grandchildren. He teaches them life lessons based on biblical principles and experience. Instead of teaching young pastors Greek or Hebrew, he teaches them grace. "They teach you those in seminary but not really the people skills you need." He continues to thank those that mentored him and is still fortunate to see many of them regularly.

Chapter Six

THANKFULNESS/APOLOGY

"Gratitude is not only the greatest of virtues, but the parent of all the others."

Cicero (106 – 43 BC)

When someone asks me "How are you doing?" I often respond with a wisecrack: "I'm vertical and have no tubes." It's not the most delicate response, but it's true— each day that I wake up next to my wife, play a game of golf, and hang out with the grandkids is a gift that I don't take for granted. We should all practice being grateful and thankful for our very existence, but surprisingly, many of us don't. As we get older, practicing gratefulness becomes even more important as each day becomes more precious than the last.

There is a fair amount of science demonstrating that thankful, appreciative people are healthier and happier than those who go through life glum and complaining. We all like to be surrounded by positive thankful people; their energy adds to ours. All of us have friends or acquaintances that complain all the time about the lack of_____ (you fill in the blank) in their lives. It would be a dull world if we were all filled with rainbows and sunshine, but it is no fun to spend time with complainers. They suck the air out of a room. During the last few years, psychologists have come to the conclusion that being thankful is not only a positive emotion, but it is probably one of the most powerful emotions. Michael McCullough, PhD, a University of Miami psychology professor who has studied thankfulness and its effects on people states, "When you are stopping and counting your blessings, you are sort of hijacking your emotional system. Thankfulness does make people happier. It's an incredible feeling." He goes on to explain that gratitude feels good because it connects us with others, and we all feel the need to be connected somehow.

Robert Emmons, PhD, a psychology professor at The University of California Davis, suggests concentrating on what life would be like without the good things, especially your loved ones. He states that grateful people "...are more alert, alive, interested, and enthusiastic, and it serves as a stress buffer as grateful people are less likely to experience envy, anger, resentment, regret, and other unpleasant emotions that produce stress."

P. Murali Doraiswany, MD, head of biologic psychology at Duke University Medical Center states, "If thankfulness were a drug, it would be the world's best-selling product with a healthy benefit for every major organ system." His research has shown measurable effects on chemical mood transmitters (serotonin and norepinephrine), reproductive hormones (testosterone), social bonding hormones (oxytocin), cognitive and pleasure-related neurotransmitters (dopamine), inflammatory and immune systems (cytokines), stress hormones (cortisol), as well as cardiac and EKG rhythms, blood pressure, and blood sugar. Wow!

A *Journal of Personality and Social Psychology* study states that grateful people report getting more sleep and better quality sleep than those who are not grateful[26]. After reading Chapter Four, in which we discuss diet, exercise, and sleep, you understand the effect of aging on health. With research now demonstrating the effect of thankfulness on health, it's time to start your journey toward a more grateful approach to life, as well as a physically healthier one.

A 2009 article on www.PsychCentral.com, "Twelve Ways to be Thankful" by Therese Borchan, sums up thankfulness with 12 simple steps. Borchan is the author of the very popular and funny book about living with depression, *Beyond Blue: Surviving Depression and Anxiety and Making the Most of Bad Genes* (Vintage Books, 2009). Her 12 steps are listed below:

---

[26] Emmons, RA, Mc McCullough, ME. "Counting Blessings Versus Burdens," *Journal of Personality and Social Psychology.* Vol 84(2): 377-389. Feb 2003.

1. See with the Heart

You must see with the heart and look at situations with the right instruments. Borchan writes, "I need to go back and tell my heart to get some guts and speak up to my head because it's starting to listen to my eyes again." In other words, left-brain analytical types are always trying to see the world through the lens of logic, reason, facts, numbers, and science, and they tend not to listen to their hearts. Thus, they miss out on doing the right thing for the right reason.

2. Change your language

Talk to yourself and to others in a different way. If you are bashing yourself or others, you cannot be grateful. Borchan writes, "If you can change your language, the seeds of gratitude will grow." It's the old conversation we have with ourselves. There is a huge difference between "I really look good in this dress. I love the color, and it fits well," versus "I love this dress because it hides my big butt." Golfers seem to stand over a ball and think of all the things that they don't want to go wrong, and I can promise that about half of those things will occur if you are thinking about them right before you hit the ball!

3. Get a gratitude partner

Borchan says that a gratitude partner is like a workout partner. Choose someone in your life who can hold you accountable for being grateful and can pull you back when anger and frustration cause you to lose sight of the positive things in your life.

4. Remember

Borchan quotes a French proverb, "Gratitude is the heart's memory." She recommends that we remember those in our lives who have walked with us and shown us kindness.

5. Keep a gratitude journal

Borchan recommends keeping a weekly or daily journal of what you are grateful for. Just like writing down what you eat helps you to reduce your overall caloric intake, writing down what you are grateful for helps serve as a useful reminder of everything you have to be grateful for. It keeps thankfulness in the forefront of your life when you sit down to think about everything you have going for you.

6. Write a thank you letter

Borchan recommends writing a letter to someone you have not properly thanked in the past, such as a parent, a relative, a mentor, a teacher, a coach, a pastor or priest, or simply a friend that has made your journey easier. If you can, read the letter to the recipient face to face. Mailing a hand-written card or letter is also a good way to express your gratitude, but steer away from e-mail and texting, as these modes of communication tend to be impersonal. (Can you imagine receiving a text message such as, "Thx for driving me to my radiation treatments"?)

7. Make a gratitude visit

Borchan explains that she makes unannounced visits to people in her life who have made a difference. She thanks these people in the presence of others. A school teacher, a professor, an employer, mentor, or friend is a good start.

8. Start a gratitude club

Borchan quotes Martin Seligman, PhD, who wrote *Authentic Happiness: Using the New Positive Psychology to Realize Your Potential for Lasting Fulfillment* (Free Press, 2003). Seligman describes a gratitude night in his classroom. He asks each student to bring someone to class and tell the class why he or she is grateful for this individual. He writes "We do not have a vehicle in our culture for letting people who mean the most to us know how thankful we are that they are on the planet."

Reading about Seligman's gratitude night reminded me of our four-year-old granddaughter, Emmy, who brought her Mimi (her grandmother and my wife) to show-and-tell at school. The rest of the class members brought sock monkeys and dolls. When the teacher asked Emmy to say something about her Mimi in front of the class, she stated in quick order, "This is my Mimi. She doesn't have a job, she has traveled all over the world, she buys me anything that I want, and she loves me." Priceless.

9. Acknowledge yourself

Write down what you have done positively for yourself. Perhaps you read a juicy novel, visited with someone who is ill or in need, took a college course, or lost weight. When you do something for someone else, it ultimately benefits you the most, so be sure to count random act of kindness.

10. Accept a gift

Borchan describes that sometimes it is difficult for people to accept a gift, especially from someone who cannot afford it. The blessing belongs to the giver—don't dampen it by refusing the gift.

11. Pray

Don't forget to say thanks.

12. Give back

If you can't thank a person who has made a difference in your life, either because he or she has passed on or because no gesture seems worthy, pay it forward. Borchan writes:

The other day I was trying to come up with a way of repaying a former professor of mine for all the encouragement and support through the years. Nothing I could ever do could match his kindness. No letter of appreciation. No visit to his classroom. So I came up with a plan: perhaps I could help some young girl who fell into my path in the same way he helped me. I told my professor friend that I would try to help and inspire this lost person. I would try to guide her to a sense of love and self-acceptance, just as he had done for me. If someone does an act of kindness for you, one way to say thanks is to do the same for another.

A. Homework: Make a Happy List

Having trouble feeling thankful? Make a happy list. Write a list of everything that makes you happy, and be sure that you experience at least one thing on that list daily. When you are done reading a page-turner, playing the piano, or volunteering at the animal shelter, take a moment to feel grateful that you are still able to do these things and recognize the contribution they make to your wellbeing.

This exercise can also work in the opposite direction. Make a list of all the things that drive you crazy, and be sure to avoid those things daily. If you engage in or experience too many things on that list in a single day, do something on the happy list as soon as you can. The happy list and crazy list are great tools to take your psychological pulse on a daily basis.

B. Caring for Aging Parents: The Ultimate Thank You

There is no higher calling than thanking your parents for all they have done for you by taking care of them as they get older. Although some are estranged from their parents or don't view them fondly, it is amazing how many children show up at the end of their parent's lives trying to make up for lost time and absolve the guilt of not visiting, calling, or sending flowers. Guilt is a terrible feeling to carry on your shoulders. Life is too short not to make amends with those who are close, and we need to continually thank those who raised us.

As our life expectancies have increased, so have the odds of needing to care for our parents as their independence wanes. According to the Association of American Retired Persons, 22 million of us are taking care of our parents. The reality is that your retirement plans may be hijacked by the financial and time constraints of taking care of elderly parents. If you find yourself in the position of taking care of aging parents, consider it a lesson in thankfulness.

As your parents age, it is important to consider three questions:

- Where will mom and dad live?
- Who will pay for their needs?
- How will I take care of myself?

Get the family in on the discussion. It probably won't be easy—your aunt may want your mom to live at home, while your brother and sister think she would be better off in an assisted living facility. Iron out these details before you are pressured by a deadline (e.g., Dad is being released from the rehabilitation facility in a week after suffering a hip fracture and can't live alone anymore).

Most importantly, include mom and/or dad in the discussion, provided they have the mental wherewithal to understand the situation and share their needs and concerns.

C. Where Will Mom and Dad Live?

Historically, generations and extensions of the same family lived in close proximity to each other, or in some cases, in the same house. But today, family members often live hundreds or thousands of miles away from each other, making the question of where mom and dad are going to live a difficult one. Most of us want to live in our own homes surrounded by our possessions and memories, but there will come a time when doing so is just not realistic. Many of my friends have built homes with a "parent" room or have remodeled existing space so their parents will have a place to live when the time comes.

If the thought of living with one or both of your parents makes you a little woozy, consider this: mom and/or dad probably don't want to live with you either. They've been doing their own thing for decades, and although you've learned to pick up your laundry and put the dishes in the sink by now, you're just as likely to cramp their style as they will cramp yours.

The new arrangement will take time and patience. Lay some ground rules to avoid getting on each other's nerves. For example, your mom may like the idea of having you in the same house for safety reasons, but she may not want you checking in on her constantly. Perhaps just a brief visit in the morning will suffice. If you are still working, hiring a home health-aid to make sure dad takes his medications and has a healthy lunch may be exactly what you need.

Another option is an assisted living facility. A lot of elderly people associate an assisted living facility with a loss of independence, and they feel it is too "institutional" to be a comfortable place to live. However, assisted living facilities often enable people to live on their own with the security of having trained professionals nearby, thus increasing their independence. An assisted living facility may offer more social opportunities for mom and dad, such as movie nights, card games, shopping trips, and even some light travel, than they would not get living in your in-law apartment. Finding the right facility will take some shopping around, and many have waiting lists, so initiate the discussion with your family now.

If mom and dad insist on living in their own home, you may just have to indulge them (unless medical needs dictate otherwise). Consider forming a circle of family, friends, and community members who can work together to provide care for your parents on a rotating schedule. Perhaps a neighbor agrees to deliver a meal once a week, your cousin agrees to mow the lawn, and your sister stops in to vacuum. Expect mom and dad to drive you at least a little crazy. Inevitably, mom will call you in a panic because the TV isn't working, and you will drive 30 minutes to her house to find that it was simply unplugged. Take these things in stride, and try to remember how nuts you drove your parents as a kid.

D. Who Will Pay for Mom and Dad's Needs?

Few things can tear a family apart quicker than money. Although mom's and dad's savings, Social Security checks, Medicare, and Medicaid will help cover some of their costs, there may be expenses that require the family to pitch in. Formulate a plan with your parents, siblings (if you have any), and professional financial advisors. Discuss their options and preferences, hopefully, before they lose their independence.

If mom and/or dad are coming to live with you, also consider the additional expense of another person or two living in the house—you may see your electricity, food, and water expenses rise. After all the dirty diapers mom changed and the hours dad spent teaching you to drive, it's not wise to ask for monetary compensation, but perhaps mom and/or dad can pitch in another way. If she is capable, mom might like to cook dinner once or twice a week, or dad might help the grandkids with their homework.

If mom and/or dad will continue living at home but need extra assistance, consider splitting the cost of a house cleaning service, meal delivery service, or home health-aid with several family members. Even a local teen from the community who can fold laundry, cook lunch, and run to the grocery store can be very helpful for an individual or couple trying to maintain their independence (and it will be a learning experience for the teen, too!).

E. How Will I Take Care of Myself?

There is no higher calling than to take care of the people you love, but it can be emotionally and financially draining. If mom and/or dad develop cognitive difficulties, you may feel like you are taking care of a small child who requires constant attention, patience, and understanding. Stay balanced. Your life is also important. If you are taking care of your parents full-time, hiring a home health-aid or other care provider to help take care of mom and dad so you can have a breather isn't a sin; neither is taking care of mom and dad from afar by contributing financially or arranging help. However you're handling the situation, be sure to feed your own soul and maintain balance (see Chapter Two). Go for a long bike ride in the mornings to clear your head, socialize with your peers, and engage in other activities that rejuvenate you.

Taking care of mom and dad may get you thinking about your own wishes as you age. Consult your children, friends, spouse, and financial advisors to map out a plan. Make a living will and give power of attorney to an individual who you trust will follow your wishes. Consider long-term care insurance if you are financially able, as it removes a huge burden from those who will be tasked with your care. Consider what you want to have happen with your house and belongings should you need to move into an assisted living facility or nursing home. You never know when your independence will be lost, so plan accordingly.

F. Speak Now or Forever Hold your Peace: Learning to Apologize

Thankfulness and apologies both require action on your part. Most of us have been thinking and functioning with our left brain (analytical, statistical, objective) and sometimes irrespective of our hearts. Retirement is a good time to get the right brain up and running. For the most part, thankfulness and apologies may be retrospective conversations or actions, but there is no time like the present to begin using right-brain emotional intelligence to thank those who have or are currently helping you. Sincere apologies also require the use of your empathetic brain. Both have huge positive effects for both the giver and the receiver.

Admitting when we are wrong is tough, but life is too short to carry around regret, so it's time to practice apologizing. Consider someone you may have wronged in the past, such as an employee, a friend, a spouse, a parent, or anyone who you may have disappointed with your actions or words. An immediate apology is obviously the best kind, but again, this is about your new and different life in retirement, so why not clean up the past one while you're at it?

The ninth of the 12 Alcoholics Anonymous steps states, "We make amends to such people whenever possible, except when to do so would injure them or others." You will not and should not try to apologize for every wrong you've ever committed (no one has enough days left). Instead, apologize to the people whose image keeps you up at night, even if you have to track them down.

Apologies require good judgment and a careful sense of timing and prudence. Timing is everything. If you are still screaming at each other and neither one of you is listening, then the apology will fall on deaf ears. Leave the room, collect your thoughts, script what you are going to say and why and then apologize. Never go to bed with an angry heart. Try not to wait until the morning to make it right. People in substance abuse recovery are encouraged to make amends for those they have injured, but again this cannot be done effectively until some time has passed and the wreckage that was left behind has had some time to heal and recover.

Sincere comes from two Greek words: "sin" means "without" and "cere" means "wax." Thus, the word means without wax. In the Greek culture, earthen vases were made of clay, painted, and sold at local markets. Artisans often filled any cracks with wax and then painted the vase to disguise the imperfections. The savvy buyer would place a candle inside the vase, and if it was "sincere," the light would not shine through. Of course, we all have cracks, but that doesn't mean we can't be sincere. If you don't truly wish to make amends with someone you've wronged, then don't do it just to check an item off of your to-do list. For your apology to be effective it must come from the heart—the person should feel your desire to make right.

I remember a patient of mine who was very upset with a surgical procedure I had performed to bone graft her severely atrophic lower jaw. The procedure left her with a partially numb lower lip on one side. This possibility was explained in detail several times prior to surgery and was written in the informed consent document that she signed. She came in one day after the procedure and told me she was going to sue me. She continued to come in for her post-operative visits, and we continued to discuss the numb lip and what could and could not be done about it. One day, about six months after the procedure, she stated, "I have decided to not sue you after all, but all I wanted was for you to say you were sorry." At that time, medical malpractice attorneys were adamant that you never told a patient you were sorry because they viewed it as an admission of guilt. Thankfully, that has now changed, and apology and full disclosure have become the standard of care. The patient and I had a tearful discussion about her lip, I apologized, and she never brought up again.

The elements of a good apology should include remorse, acceptance of responsibility, admission of wrong doing, acknowledgment of harm, a promise to behave better, a request for forgiveness, and an offer of repair. It can be difficult to repair a wrong that occurred in the distant past, but there may have been a hurtful action or word that you regret and can't seem to forget, so why not try? If it is not well received, then at least the effort has been good for you.

In an October 18, 2010 *Wall Street Journal* article, Elizabeth Bernstein described the various types of apologies. The first type is the most effective.

1.) The heartfelt apology: A completely earnest and well intentioned mea culpa, demonstrating that you both understand and regret the pain you inflicted. It sounds like this: "I am sorry. I understand that I hurt you. It won't happen again."

2.) The strategic apology: A not entirely sincere apology, offered to end a fight and to stop the other person from hurting. You may not feel that what you did was wrong. "I'm sorry. Let's move on."

3.) The defensive apology: This is a self-protecting, half-baked (and therefore rarely effective) maneuver meant to defend your actions as much as offer contrition. "I'm sorry, but_____."

4.) The contingent apology: This apology is used when you want to appease a person but don't know what you have done wrong, or don't care. "If" is the key word here. "I am sorry if I have done something wrong."

5.) The too-late apology: This is an expression of regret that comes days, months, or even years too late. "I realize that what I did was wrong." Too-late apologies have a place if they are sincere, so why not give it a shot?

Regardless of how sincere your apology, the person you are apologizing to may not forgive you. If this is the case, accept it and move on. You've said your piece, tried your best, and now it's up to the individual to forgive you or forget you. Respect his or her choice. You may also encounter more anger than you were expecting or learn that your past actions had a deeper effect on the person's life than you ever intended. Perhaps firing Betty instead of taking the time to mentor her ultimately led to her home's foreclosure when she couldn't find other work. Maybe an off-handed remark to Bill was the straw that broke the camel's back and crushed his confidence in the workplace. Be prepared for less-than-pleasant reactions without getting defensive.

When possible, apologize in person. Making the effort to get together with the person and saying what you need to say in his or her presence is infinitely more meaningful than an e-mail that took fewer than five minutes to write. If the person lives too far away for you to apologize in person, or if you do not think the person would be receptive to a phone call, it may be appropriate to hand-write a note of apology. Include your phone number to invite the person to talk it over if he or she wishes.

Jim Schierling, the Bible Church pastor we met in Chapter Five, continues to ask for forgiveness when he has spoken or acted without thinking. He states he has had a "lifetime habit of asking for forgiveness as soon as he learns he has offended someone." He states that his most common thoughtless remarks are unintentional hurts. Through the years, his wife has taught him to think about the effect of an honest remark before hurting someone. "Grace is much more of a motivator than guilt. The correct attitude that leads to action is a guiding principle based on God's teaching of grace."

The point of all of this is to make apology and admitting when you are wrong part of your thinking. Many of us go through the majority of our lives without being able to admit that we were wrong, rash, or just plain stupid. Some of us are not very good at admitting when we fall outside of the rigid boundaries we set for ourselves, but this skill can save relationships, mend past hurts, and help you start this next chapter of your life with a clean slate.

A friend of mine, Norb Walters, said to me, "Words really don't work—your actions are what count. You apologize by changing." If you can't apologize in person or the individual isn't receptive to your apology, balance the karmic scales by doing a good deed for another person. If you fired Betty, make it a goal to help someone else land his or her dream job. If your words were hurtful, pass kind words onto someone else. It may not be the resolution you were looking for, but you will get better sleep at night.

G. Norb's Story: The Joy of Giving

Norb Walter retired at age 62. He is now 71, but he looks 50. He has a business degree from Michigan State University and was the vice president of sales and marketing of Alcon Laboratories. During his working years, he was a "24-hour kind of guy" and was nearly always the boss. After he retired and didn't have an office to go to every day, he struggled. He spent an entire career setting goals for himself and others and enjoyed helping his subordinates achieve their goals as well. He did not state the fact, but it is obvious that he is a great mentor.

When he finally stopped working, Norb was in need of new goals and places to go. He has been married for 52 years and quickly realized that staying home all the time would drive both he and his wife crazy. He is a big-idea kind of guy and continues to promote ideas, products, and people, and he raises money for Youth Education Town, a charity sponsored by the National Football League that builds recreation and education centers in the inner cities.

One day, I overheard him talking about football tickets he gave away. I asked him to elaborate for me. A young man who is a locker room attendant at the athletic club that Norb frequents was talking about his dad being a big Dallas Cowboy fan. Norb gave the attendant four 50-yard-line seats so that the young man could take his dad to a Cowboy game on his birthday. The pleasure of giving was evident as Norb told the story.

Chapter Seven
LEGACY/LEFTOVERS

"What you leave behind is not what is engraved in stone on a monument, but what is woven into the lives of others."

Pericles (495-429 BC)

The question of what you would like your legacy to be is the toughest of all the questions you've had to consider thus far as you plan for or begin your retirement. It is probably the most reflective question on my personal list. Many of us have not given our legacies much thought, and when we do, we naturally think we are taking ourselves too seriously. But everyone leaves a legacy, whether you intend to or not, so you might as well make it a good one. I suspect most of you have left a legacy in your pre-retirement career, but your legacy after you start your retirement may just be the one that sticks.

A. Consider Your Legacy

Many of us are complacent in that we tend to think about only ourselves and the present. "What do I need to do today, and how am I going to accomplish it?" is the first thing many of us think when we wake up in the morning, but I would encourage all of us to take time and have the courage to reflect on the future and the individuals who will follow in our footsteps. It's going to take some guts to think about your own demise; it might be painful, but it may help you shape how you live the rest of your life.

I suggest revisiting Chapter Two, which discusses the balance equation: family, work, recreation, and spirituality. We leave a legacy in all four areas. Take, for example, the legacy my parents left behind. You can't choose your family, but if it was possible, mine would have been a great choice. I was fortunate to have two loving parents who were exceptionally grounded in the principles of balance. They worked, but it was really a means to an end for them. Their primary focus was the family, spiritual matters, and recreation as a family. My dad, who taught Bible study classes for 40 years, was one of those guys who had it all together; he had a great sense of humor, self-deprecating at times. His stories were always funny and had a point or a lesson in them. His character was impeccable, above reproach, and he was the most transparent and honest man I have ever known. He loved to have a good time, but it always included the entire family. Both my parents lived and modeled a life of grace in which our humanity was recognized. Growing up, I learned that we would fail at times, disappoint at times, but we would always be forgiven. Their love for each other and for my sister and me was unconditional. We never had a lot of money, but we lived a very rich life.

Our vacations were camping trips (in a tent) in Colorado, Wyoming, New Mexico and the east coast. We visited nearly all the states as a family, traveling by car. Instead of sending us to camp, we all went camping. We learned to share, build a fire, cook over a fire, fish for trout, enjoy the outdoors, and appreciate simple games. We learned to play dominoes, and later bridge, in a tent at night under a lantern. Instead of sending me to golf or tennis camp, Dad taught me both and played with me. He was a great friend. We were ranked third in the state in father-son doubles in tennis at one time. He taught sportsmanship by example.

My parents' legacy has been a driving force throughout my life. I have tried to emulate my parents' parenting skills when we raised our three daughters, and now I try to at least passively transfer them to our grandchildren. My wife and I would load all the girls in a van every summer for a couple of weeks to see the country. The girls really hated being crammed in a van with each other for the first day, but at the end of the trip, each girl was able to communicate better with her sisters, my wife, and I, and I dare say they appreciated each other and their parents more. The girls remain close friends and communicate with each other almost daily. Their mother is also their friend. I truly want the legacy that my parents left me to be perpetual. I am starting to see my children passing down these traditions and behaviors to their young families. Leaving a legacy is a big-picture thing, expansive, imaginative, and meaningful.

I asked Lou Hendricks the former CIA division chief, about his legacy. He thought a moment and simply said "I just want to be remembered as a patriot." Jim Rickman, my engineer friend, said his legacy is that his children are kind and caring.

When I asked myself the same question, I was tempted to answer that it would be all the good I did in 28 years of practice, but I suspect most of my patients would not even remember my name. I always wanted to be an educator and flirted several times with leaving private practice and becoming a professor in an oral and maxillofacial residency training program. The chips never fell into place, and the legacy I had intended for myself went by the wayside. I'm still not quite sure how I will answer this question for myself, but I think that ultimately, my answer will include the guidance I provide to medical staffs that are struggling with disruptive physicians and the mentoring work I'm doing now.

Many years ago, I received a call from the superintendent of our local school system asking if I could have lunch to discuss his son's career plans. His son was in college at the time. I encouraged the young man to consider dentistry, specifically oral and maxillofacial surgery, as an option and recommended he obtain a medical degree along the way. Several years later, I heard he was training in oral and maxillofacial surgery in San Antonio. My colleagues and I came to a point in our practice where we needed to add a fourth surgeon, and I asked our most recent partner who he would choose. He gave me the name of the young man I had directed into oral surgery; I had no idea they even knew each other. The young man came to the practice about the time I had to retire. He stayed a year and then pursued a full-time academic career to teach other oral and maxillofacial surgeons at Southwestern Medical School and later, in Jackson, Mississippi. He told me not long ago that my encouragement and advice led to his career choice. He said "I am teaching in your place." So, although I never got a chance to become a professor in an oral and maxillofacial residency program, my legacy has fulfilled that desire.

As I've mentioned, Saundra Marling, author of *Boomer's Job Search Guide: You're Not Old, You're Experienced,* and her husband Carl, a talented ophthalmologist, are good friends of mine. When we discussed legacy,

Saundra said women view legacy differently than men. Women tend to think of their legacies in terms of their children, while men tend to think of their legacies in terms of worldly accomplishments, titles, money, and prestige in addition to family. For example, Carl thought his practice and the building he built to house it would be a lasting legacy, but he is finding out that neither will last long after he retires. Saundra's legacy is built around her children and grandchildren.

People who do not have children may have nieces and nephews they are close to or consider a cause dear to their hearts their "baby." For example, most of the female physicians I know who do not have children tend to consider the children they see at homeless shelters, shelters for abused women, mission trips, and charity clinics their "children." We all have children; they may just not be biological.

B. Exercises to Help you Find Your Personal Legacy

Some people may already know what they want their legacy to be, but if you're not one of them, consider the following exercises to help you articulate it:

C. Write Your Own Obituary:

Most of one's legacy is unintentional and not known to until after death. You don't get to write your own obituary, but you probably don't want it to be all about your work, positions, and accolades. I scan the obituary page in our local paper every day, mainly to see if I know anyone, but my wife *reads* them. We have found that ordinary people accomplish extraordinary things, and who we consider extraordinary people just did ordinary things. What do you want your obituary to say? It sounds like a morbid exercise, but it may help you decide what you want your legacy to be. Do you want it to say "He was chairman of ABC Company," or do you want it to explain how you took time to volunteer, teach, and serve others? Sit down, start writing, and see what comes of it.

D. Get Back to Your Roots

Another great legacy project is to trace your family background to its roots. If there is a culture, heritages, or a tradition from your roots, make it a priority to explain and model it for your children, grandchildren, and others in your community. For example, bring a traditional dish to the dinner table; introduce a budding musician in the family to folk music from the country that your parents and grandparents originate; or celebrate little known holidays (e.g., if you're French, whip out the sparklers on Bastille Day, or if you're Canadian, cook up a Thanksgiving feast in October).

One of my nieces traced our family back to John Howland, who came over on the Mayflower. He is the one who fell off the ship, married his boss, and eventually had a great deal of influence in the New World. A great exercise is to interview your parents or surviving relatives concerning your origins. This will not only help you understand the legacy that your forefathers and foremothers have left you, but it will also help shape your vision of the legacy you want to leave the younger generations. Tracing genealogy has become a growth industry, and there are many Web sites than can help you with your quest. When your research is complete, the resulting family history is a great way to explain to your children and grandchildren how, where, and from whom they came from. We all need connections, even if some are injurious.

Tracing your genealogy can also be therapeutic. I help run educational/therapy sessions for physicians struggling with addictions, and a helpful exercise is to draw a family origin diagram. The participants explain their family trees to a small group of attendees, and the insight that is derived from this project is rewarding, insightful, and revealing. It is particularly helpful to those who have a strong family background of addiction because it helps explain their disease and how the course of their lives turned out as it has—at least one aspect of their chaotic lives isn't their fault. The opposite is also true: strong family roots that are positive and uplifting tend to provide perspective to those who are struggling with feeling alone or without a safety net. Most of the time, of course, there is a mixture of each.

All generations are self-centered and focused on today and tomorrow, and that is a good thing, but what a blessing to have reminders of your heritage from those who came before.

E. Vern's Story: Balancing the Karmic Scales by Creating a New Legacy

Vern Oechsle, a Harvard MBA with an accounting background, became president of a large automobile component company at age 37 and was responsible for 25,000 employees. He later became a manager at Allied Signal and was responsible for 40,000 employees. He was considered a "slice and dice" guy, which meant his expertise was in downsizing to make the manufacturing units more profitable. Upper management changed, and he was given his golden parachute at age 48.

Vern got bored pretty quickly. He rearranged the house, the kitchen, and anything else he could get his hands on until his wife told him to get out of the house more. At the age of 51, he became CEO of a $2 billion steel company in Houston after interviewing for 60 positions. He made it until age 58 at that company before he decided to take an early retirement. He never regretted it, and wished he had stopped working sooner.

With his newly found freedom, he took woodworking classes and went to Arizona for a two-week cowboy college course. He came back to Texas and bought land, cattle, and horses. He began making furniture for his children and has become much more conscious of the many poor and needy people in the community. He encouraged his daughter and granddaughter to work at the food pantry distribution site at a local church. It has been an eye-opening experience and humbling for the whole family. The church's facilities are old and falling apart, so Vern's daughter volunteered him to hang some cabinets. It soon turned into a weekly assignment, as the church keeps coming up with more work for him.

Vern has done several projects for the very needy clients who come to the church every Tuesday for free food as well. The need for knowledgeable, able people who can help these very poor folks is incredible, and Vern is happy to do what he can. After a career of putting a lot of people on the street and closing their places of employment, Vern takes great satisfaction in being able to give back a little and help those who need it.

The lesson that Vern learned was that the past does not matter; you must close one chapter and open another. He had never really thought about a legacy, but at this age, his family is his number one legacy. He wants to be known as hard-working, honest, simple, and as someone who does not play favorites.

F. There are no luggage racks on hearses

Leftovers are what we find at estate and garage sales, and I hate garage sales. I once offered my wife a large sum of money if she would not have a garage sale. Of course, she made more money than I offered, but it was disheartening to think that she sold $10,000 worth of stuff for about $300. I am a traditionalist and sentimental to a fault. I understand things are just things, and there are no luggage racks on hearses.

In her early 90s, my mother starting cleaning out her house by giving her treasures to her grandchildren. She is blessed to have seen all of her grandchildren grow into adulthood. She knows each of the five pretty well, their interests, and their connections to the past. She began to give each of them "treasures" from her past. Some belonged to her mother, some belonged to her, and some had belonged to my dad. She gave each grandchild photographs and the stories behind them, so they would have a better understanding of where they came from. She explained the significance of each gift and why it was important to her. None of her valuables were valuable in a monetary sense, but her gesture was meaningful for the five grandchildren and her. Her planning and insight saved us a lot of time and angst. Enjoy your things as long as you are able, but make sure they find an appropriate home where they will be loved and used when your time comes.

Another approach to handling the leftovers is to have a croak box. When my friend Gary Reeves died, his son called me and said they had opened his croak box. I asked "quote box?" and his son said, "No, his croak box!" Gary made a box that he labeled "croak box," which was to be opened when he died. It had instructions of who to call first, second, and third. It had what songs he wanted sung at his funeral and why. It included who he would like to speak at his funeral and who he wanted his pall bearers to be. He had taken the time to list what he wanted each of his children and grandchildren to have on his passing and why. Of course you should probably have this information in a last will and testament, but a croak box is practical, immediate, and personal.

I still cling to the idea that who we become is to some degree determined by our heritage and legacy of our parents and grandparents. This can be present in beliefs and values, but also can be manifested in material treasures. Take time to think about what items you would like to leave behind (you can't take any with you), and explain why it is important to you and why you think it will be important to the recipient. Why not give the stuff away before they put you away?

I would challenge each of you to ask yourself, "What would I like my legacy to be?" It is never too late to make a difference.

Chapter Eight
PERSONAL REFLECTIONS

"A leader is a man who can adapt principles to circumstances."

Gen. George C. Patton

(1885-1945)

I hope by now you realize that there is life after retirement, and you have control over that life. Just meet Harry and the two Bobs; their retirement stories show that you can be just as successful at retirement as you were in your day job, if not more so.

A. Harry Karegeannes' Story

Harry Karegeannes, a retired Major General in the U.S. Army, has a master's degree in acquisition management from the Florida Institute of Technology and is a western historian and firearms expert of some renown. Harry and I started hunting birds together several years ago with two other men. George Akin held the same rank that Harry did in the Army prior to his retirement and continued to be called General Akin until his death. Harry was the opposite of George in that regard—he liked to be called just "Harry." Both were tried and true leaders of the first order. The other man in our hunting group was Gary Reeves, who had a PhD in engineering from Texas A&M and recently passed away. This was a pretty head-strong group. We had no followers, only leaders, but George always took command. Harry personifies humility, and his story is meaningful because it describes why I thought this book would be helpful to those who had highly functioning positions and then were put out to pasture.

The four of us would have long and sometimes passionate discussions about the state of the world, who had the best shot (that would have been Gary), religion, politics, sports (usually the state of the Dallas Cowboys and the Texas A&M Aggies), where we were going to hunt next, what time we were going to leave in the morning, and anything else we could think of. The late-night discussions usually involved a bottle of single malt scotch. The most interesting and compelling discussions had to do with leadership. I was always of the opinion that leaders were born, not made, but I came to agree with the two generals that true leaders can be taught their craft. Harry share's his story:

To put things into perspective, I spent 34 years in the army and then worked in the corporate world at Lockheed Marin, the world's largest defense company, for 10 years before really retiring. I had three major life transitions to deal with: from military to civilian to retiree.

My last job in the Army was as the Commanding General of the Army's Depot Systems Command (DESCOM).This was the largest logistical organization in the services at that time. DESCOM was composed of 13 major depots (storage facilities for weapons, tank, cars, etc.) and 27 smaller depot activities, primarily in the US, but also in Germany, Korea, and during Desert Storm (1991), in Saudi Arabia. I would equate this go of command and management to that of the CEO of a relatively large company. My job was to insure that we provided the best, most timely and economical wholesale support of material needed by our armed forces in the pursuit of their missions during war or peace.

In industry, I began as the Director of Material (this is all subcontracting) for the missile division of Lockheed Martin. I was later promoted to vice president of materials and facilities responsible for all subcontracting and the general infrastructure of the company. I had approximately 500 employees in my organization.

Transitioning to civilian life from the Army after 34 years was difficult. I went from being a relatively successful, high-level leader of a major organization to a mid-level manager in a highly competitive industry where my peers were significantly younger than me. Once I was promoted to vice president, I felt better about the transition, as I was back in a high-level position. I found out that while I was serving "on freedom's frontiers," these younger folks in industry were earning twice my pay plus amenities, such as stock options and bonuses. One does not serve in the military for the money—the only profits paid by the Army are in increased security, mission accomplishment, and the very important honor of leading America's fine young men and women. There is nothing in industry that equates to the feeling of satisfaction that is derived from that experience.

I was taken aback by the vast differences in the value systems of the military versus those I found in industry. It may sound maudlin, but I truly believed in "God, duty, honor, and country" while I was in the service. I found that industry was driven by the bottom line and the profits that were to be made. That should not have surprised me, but I did not realize how pervasive that motivation was. The application of the basic principles of leadership, which seemed natural to me, was not as readily evident in industry. This was always a concern to me, and I came close several times to ending my career in the corporate environment either voluntarily or because I had offended someone higher up.

I found that many of the bosses in the corporate structure who were great engineers or analysts were poor leaders. They never did quite understand the difference between managing a program and leading people through personal example or by interfacing with their workers.

It came as a shock to me to realize that Lockheed Martin paid me for everything. This included very nice stock options and bonuses. I joke that the only option the Army ever gave me was smoking or non-smoking. I was somewhat amused with the bosses in industry who agonized constantly over developing leaders and leadership skills. Many never quite understood that there is a vast difference between managing and leading. I recall a time when the Lockheed Martin president was discussing one of his "great ideas." He was going to select the top 250 employees with the most potential for future growth and leadership roles and develop programs to speed their advancement and promotion. I said that that did not sound like a good approach to me (I had become more diplomatic in my comments over the years). I explained that if he proceeded with this plan, he will essentially tell the remaining 3,500 employees that they are considered "also ran," second-rate employees who will not be selected for the good things of tomorrow in this company. He agreed that a better approach would be to allow each VP to select and nurture employees based on performance promote them based on the future succession needs of the various organizations within the company, such as the engineering department, the materials department, etc.

In retrospect, although the Army gave me a clear perspective of how to motivate people, values, methods of leadership, caring for soldiers, and how to develop plans and courses of action to accomplish an objective, industry gave me the chance to use much of that knowledge and offered a degree of financial security I would never have attained from my military career.

When I finally retired and came home to stay, I had the toughest time transitioning so far. It was difficult to wake up and realize that I had no meetings, conferences, or decisions to make other than those associated with my life at home. As I was preparing to leave the Army, an associate who was a very successful businessman asked me, "Harry, how will it feel to go from being the 'big daddy' to being nothing?" I scoffed at him and found that going directly into a defense job made that transition a bit easier. However, when I retired, his comments took on a new meaning.

When I retired, I had already passed the legendary 65-year milestone, so my life has not been filled with cruise ships, reunions, and such. My age coupled with some family members' health problems have kept me fairly close to home. I am afraid that my wife and I went through major adjustments during my first year at home, mainly due to my being there all the time. The struggle was finally resolved as I became more involved in reading, became somewhat proficient on the computer, and started writing articles for a collector's magazine, but mostly because of our enduring love, patience, and understanding. I became more involved with several tasks that allowed me to contribute some time, leadership, and management skills, including becoming president of the home owner's association, president of the church council, a member of the planning committee for building a new church, and other community posts. I do this not to ensure a place in afterlife, but because I can contribute something in the present life.

To keep myself busy and challenged, I lean heavily on my hobbies, such as antique arms restoration, research, and collecting interesting historical pieces. I wrote several articles for arms collector magazines but finally decided that it was too time-consuming and expensive, so I focused on spending more time with my family, which was long overdue. I have used my leadership training and skills to mentor others over the years. I learned early on that one of the most effective methods of mentoring is by personal example.

I was blessed with some very fine friends, both new ones and those from my past, who made retirement more meaningful and enjoyable. Hunting friends were an important part of this. As we grew older, we all came to believe that sharing the time together meant more than the hunting itself.

Family also grew to be more important as the years passed and loved ones began to leave us. The same goes for cherished friends. Each one who died left (and continues to leave) a vacant place in my heart. The actress Betty Davis once said, "Getting old ain't for sissies"! She was dead on!

One of my real regrets, and one that I know most of us would agree on, is that I have lost touch with so many friends and associates. I did not make the effort to keep in touch. Those special people who took time to mentor and help me during my early years are in my mind a lot more, and I wish I had done more to let them know how much they meant to me over the years. This includes my brothers, father, mother, in-laws, and a passel of others in uniform and out.

I would like to believe that I thanked those people I needed to thank at the time. I believe that I tried to recognize and reward deserving individuals over the years, but I recognize that I could have done more. Being busy is not an excuse for failing to do what is right. For example, I did not give my wife the recognition she certainly earned and deserved, especially during that very demanding lifestyle that you encounter in the military. Also, I should have fought harder to see to it that outstanding subordinates were promoted and recognized for their achievements.

One danger of being alone is that you can become distressed over the reality that you no longer are a part of or important to the process, whatever it may be. I find that I need more time alone to enjoy my areas of interest and to consider the issues of the world, but I do still miss participating in the various aspects of commanding and managing an organization with challenging tasks and missions—both military and civilian. One interesting aspect of this struggle is that I have numerous, detailed dreams in which I am involved in decision making, commanding, and problem solving. These are not negative or nightmarish in nature, but they are similar to past experiences that I have participated in. In some of these excursions, I am in charge, and in others, I am a participant.

So that I am not completely alone, I got a dog. I found that having a good dog gives me great happiness. My dog motivates me to get out and walk. Keeping physically fit certainly is important to your body as well as your mental well-being after retirement.

If I were to give advice to baby boomers about to retire, I'm not sure I could keep the list concise because there are too many things to consider. My list includes:

- *Don't believe all that stuff that folks tell you about your importance to the organization, etc. Take the compliments but temper them with reality. In other words, the company or organization you were a big part of won't fall apart when you're gone. It may change, but it probably won't die.*

- *Accept that the time to go comes to all of us.*
- *Whatever you figure that you will need in the way of financial support for your retirement, double it. That is the amount you can live on if you have resolved your housing situation by paying off your mortgage or having a payment so low that it does not jeopardize your future retirement income.*
- *Talk out all your concerns, plans, and situation with your spouse and loved ones before retirement.*
- *Keep busy and make a contribution where ever you can.*
- *Keep physically fit.*
- *Get a good dog.*
- *Keep your self-respect.*
- *Take the time to relax with a good book and with good friends whenever you can.*
- *Remember, there ain't no bad scotch, some is just better than others!*

- *Take the time to do the things you always wanted to do as much as you can.*
- *Be sure that you have all your legal matters in good shape. Have your will, military discharge papers, insurance policies and such centrally located in a good fire proof safe so that your spouse or whomever you choose can have immediately access. Keep it current.*
- *Do not get old too fast.*

Ask yourself, "If I had it to do over again, would I change anything in my retirement?" I have always regretted that I did not buy 100 acres of land in west Texas as a retreat and a place to spend time with my friends and family members. I also would have left my corporate job a lot sooner if I had it all to do over again.

Overall, I can't complain and am thankful to God for all his blessings, allowing me to have good health, good friends, a loving family, and to have served with some of our finest young men and women as well as many great leaders and

devoted patriots.

B. Bob Karper's Story

Bob Karper is a close friend of mine. We have a lot in common, but disagree on most everything. I think he thinks he is an attorney, not a physician. We worked together for many years in hospital leadership and held the same positions at different times over the years. His passion for excellence and understanding of the human spirit on the job was unparalleled. We struggled together when dealing with disruptive and impaired physicians; we probably made more enemies than friends, but tried to always have patient safety as our primary goal. We retired the same month from the hospital where we both worked and had the privilege of leading the medical staff. I think his answers really reflect, for the most part, what this book is about: being able and prepared to step into your new role with different goals, all the time not agonizing over what you used to do. Bob shares his story:

I was the medical director of a hospital laboratory. As such, I provided the hospital with pathologists and was their representative to the hospital administration. I was responsible for organizing and operating the group both medically and financially. As director of the clinical lab, I was responsible for keeping the lab accurate, medically relevant, timely, and responsive to the medical staff. I had the ultimate responsibility for the medical aspects of the lab to the medical staff.

As an anatomic pathologist, I examined tissue removed from the hospital's patients. I also served as vice president of a larger group of pathologists, of which our group in the hospital was a part. I was active in the hospital medical staff and chaired all of their committees at one time or another. I served as credentials committee chair for 15 years because of a steadfast belief that working with high quality physicians is highly rewarding, and it is professionally and financially dangerous working with poor ones. I served as chief of staff for two years and served on the hospital's board of trustees, the hospital system's board of trustees, and the system's physician leadership council. I served as chair of the physician assistance committee for the last several years and dealt with physicians who suffered from substance abuse, emotional problems, or health issues, including aging.

I'm not sure I have learned much from retirement except how busy you can be with nothing to do. I planned fairly carefully for retirement, and so far it has proceeded accordingly and on my schedule (thank you, Lord). I saved money, never spent more than I earned, took good care of myself so I could enjoy my retirement, and took more time off as retirement approached. In my later years, I took progressively longer vacations, and retirement has proved to be just a long vacation without pay. I was a little surprised how easily life went on at the office without me. It confirmed my previous experience that we are all here for a surprisingly short time, and life is pretty much what we make of it while we are here. Nothing we did during our careers is going to last a significant amount of time (geologically speaking) and life goes on at the office.

When I retired, I'm not sure I had any major adjustments to make with my wife. I can't say the same for her. She was pretty much used to doing as she pleased without my input other than having dinner on the table at 6:30 every night. I worked, and she took care of everything else. She was alone most of the day, quietly doing her work without interference. Now I'm home wanting to know what she is doing, wanting to talk, and making a mess. She has not retired from her work and has had to help me readjust our workload. She has had to reiterate to me several times "I don't work for you, remember!"

I spent most of my professional life in the future and the present. Legacy for me is the past, and I have never thought about it. I just hope I was successful at what I tried to be and good at whatever I do. In my various administrative roles, I caused a number of people significant angst and probably pain. I hope in retrospect, they believe I behaved professionally and with care and fairness even though I'm relatively sure they didn't like what I did. I have fired people (or caused them to be fired), removed physicians' privileges, removed physicians and other professionals from the medical staff, sent people to counseling and rehab against their will, and other acts that caused mayhem and financial loss in someone's life. I did it all with what I hope was a clear *moral compass with the patient's (or group's) best interest at the center.*

The only legacy I really care about is what my kids and grandkids think of me, and I am still working on that. It is probably the only legacy that will last any significant amount of time. If you ask my ex-coworkers what they think my legacy is, they would probably ask "Who are you talking about?"

Balance has always been of major importance to me. I was miserable in medical school when all I did was work. There was no time for anything else. Once I began practicing, I always took vacations and had lots of interests outside of work. I'm certain I didn't spend enough time with my family, or maybe I was fortunate and kept out of my wife's way because my kids turned out great, I'm still married to the same woman, and I'm close to my sisters and their families. Not much has changed except I have closed the doctor book and opened the family and friends book wider.

I probably should send a few thank you notes to those who have helped me over the years, but I tried very hard to show my appreciation at the time something occurred. However, most of the people around me said I was too quick to criticize and too slow to praise. I worked to correct that in my later years and made a little progress. The only note I should write is to my longtime physician partner who I deeply respect and love dearly. We could have been much better friends, but I always had my medical director hat on. There is no question in my mind that I "rode him too hard," and didn't listen and praise enough.

My advice for other baby boomers is don't hang up your spurs until you have to or want to. I know people on both sides. Some view work as painful and can't wait to quit, while others couldn't stand to give it up. I have a dentist friend who would go crazy if he couldn't go into the office. It seems to be too much a part of who he is and his social network. Those who found work painful, in my experience, have not had a problem in retirement and appear to prosper as long as the finances work. To those like my dentist friend, I would suggest they plan for it, because working successfully until you clutch your chest and die in the saddle rarely pans out. Unless you plan, it is more likely life will show you the exit at stage left. That usually is some horrible event, and then you have to deal with the event in addition to shutting down your work life, like a doctor friend of mine who went straight from work to the Alzheimer's unit. I don't think he hurt anyone because, as you know, medicine is an over-learned skill that is late to go, but it sure was a mess for his kids, not to mention his legacy.

Now that I am retired, not only am I okay with being myself, but I love it. Working and being what someone else wants you to be (or what you think they want you to be) is hard. Being yourself is easy. Being old and retired, in some ways, makes it easier to not care if "yourself" doesn't please everyone. I have significantly mellowed with age, but not with retirement. I'm just trying to beat my friends in golf. I've significantly lowered my standards. Those high standards were in the doctor book.

C. Bob Thompson's story

Bob Thompson is living the dream, and his story is the perfect example of the fact that one does not have to hang up the spurs at the retirement party. Bob decided not to hang on to a job that was quickly becoming obsolete and literally sailed off into the sunset.

I was a civil engineer, vice-president of a prominent Texas consulting engineering firm, and head of the dam design department. I managed projects through the study stage, presentations, permitting, design, and bidding, and I represented the client during construction. I performed safety analysis of existing dams and oversaw rehabilitation if needed.

I had been with the firm for 36 years, and environmental issues had just about stopped the construction of new dams, so I was becoming obsolete. I had a dream of going sailing and did not want to change my engineering specialty. I was 58, and it was time to step aside and let the younger engineers take control. I did not want to just hang on for the sake of money and prestige. I determined how much money was enough to do what I wanted and cut myself free from a paycheck and bonuses. I never regretted it. Jill (my wife) participated in this decision and was willing to give it a try.

When I first met Jill (I was 52 and twice divorced), I told her of my plans to retire and sail around the world. She was from Oklahoma and not too sure about living on the ocean. We chartered bare-boats in the Caribbean together, and she gained confidence in both me and herself. We agreed to try it for a year to see how we got along. If it worked out, we would cross the Atlantic. As Gary Reeves said, "bad breath is better than no breath at all!" We found that we could live in close quarters together and not compete. We developed respect for each other's abilities, trusted each other's judgment, and became a team. My dream became our project, our adventure. Our relationship continued to improve.

We lived on our sailboat for 10 years, seven of which were spent in Northern Europe. The experience of living in that culture changed me. I moved to the left politically. I would come home to Texas each year to see my financial advisor, the doctor, and my accountant and do some work for my firm (They kept me on a leave of absence as long as I could be carried on their medical insurance program.).

When we visited home, it seemed like everybody was in a mad quest for "more." No one was asking how much is enough? The social system was a disaster. We were the richest country in the world, and there were homeless people on the street begging for food! The separation of the haves and have-nots was increasing. We had changed and our friends had not. They were content with the status quo or could not see the change in the country. We felt like we did not belong in Texas anymore. I have four children scattered around the world, so there was no reason to return to Texas, especially since I had become a Democrat!

We thought we would settle on the coast, near the ocean, but property values were too high, the place was crowded, and people were building on the wreckage of Hurricane Hugo. We had developed a check list of what to look for in a place to retire. We drove through Brevard, NC on a trip to Texas and liked the forest and mountains. It was July 4th, and Main St. was closed off for a craft show and celebration. We loved it and came back for a longer visit.

We rented a house in Brevard, moved off the boat, and put her up for sale. We were operating on gut feelings when we found a house we liked in a neighborhood we liked (no gated communities for us) and bought it. Jill and I were used to moving from place to place and making new friends. My kids were used to me being gone and out of touch, so it was not a change for us to move to a strange place. Through our association with the Democratic Party and Unitarian Universalist Fellowship, we made many friends with whom we have much in common. We have been here 10 years and would not change a thing.

Now that we are back on land, I keep mentally and physically active. I enjoy woodwork and am very good at it. It gives me a chance to design a project and build it (the engineer in me). I am active in the Unitarian Universalist fellowship, which supports my spiritual program. Jill and I are very active in the county Democratic Party and have made many friends with like interests. I have been volunteering at the county library two mornings a week for the past nine years processing new books. We travel, enjoy arts and crafts, and visit my four children and two grandchildren when we can.

When I first retired, I had the feeling that I needed to be doing something all the time – keep busy, earn your keep. Crossing the Atlantic in a small sailboat taught me to relax and take life a day at a time. Life for me is much easier and more enjoyable since I retired. If there is pressure, it is of my own making. I don't enjoy or need pressure anymore. I work at my own pace.

If I had waited until I was 70 to retire, I would not have been physically able to sail across the Atlantic twice and live my dream. My advice is don't worry about having enough money, your health will probably run out first. I have encouraged others who have said "I've always dreamed of doing what you are doing," to set a date and begin planning toward that goal. It will never happen if you don't set a date. Once you do that, every decision you make – especially financial ones– supports your goal.

Chapter Nine
FICTION, FACTS, AND FINANCES

"Wise men don't need advice. Fools won't take it. Beware of the little expenses; a small leak will sink a great ship."

Benjamin Franklin (1706-1790)

My original intent was not to discuss the financial aspects of retirement, but as I continued to discuss retirement from the health and psychological standpoints, it seemed apparent that I should discuss some aspects of financial health. This chapter is not a guideline for how to invest, but I hope it will give you some thoughts and tools to work with.

Throughout my working life, I contributed to pension plans, IRAs and 401(k) s all on the advice of accountants, bankers, and financial advisors. Over the years, I used varying professionals to manage my portfolio and had accounts in several institutions. When I retired, I realized I needed quality and quantity in my approach to finances and some assurance that my wife and I would not outlive our resources. On the advice of close friends, we sought out an independent fee-for-service financial advisor to not only manage our finances, but to organize our financial life. This was a huge step. To my surprise, the fee for the independent financial advisor was the same I was paying a national brokerage firm for the advice I was not receiving. In addition, the account executive of the national brokerage firm seemed to change more often than my golf handicap. He or she always had a cool sounding name and I assume resided in or around Boston. We live in Texas. On the face of it, it really betrayed common sense to have someone 2,000 miles away taking care of my finances.

I asked David Diesslin, MBA, CFP, past president and chairman of the National Association of Personal Financial Advisors (NAPFA), and our financial advisor, to summarize his philosophy on investing during retirement and how to choose an advisor. I also asked him to elaborate some of the technical aspects of asset allocation and risk aversion. In short, balance applies as much to finances as it does to every other aspect of your life.

A. Making Money without an Income

You are now retired, you have made it, but the world has changed, and the comfort of the steady income is gone. It can be a little challenging to find balance both at home and in the community when earning a living turns into earning a return. So, how does one go about conceptualizing the financial model that will work for him or her? Think of yourself and your financial health as a business. Businesses look at ratios in four primary areas:

- Leverage: Leverage is your ability to borrow based on past and current credit ratings. In retirement, that probably should be limited to appreciating assets or those that are tax deductible, such as a home mortgage.

- Liquidity: Liquidity pertains to assets that can be easily converted to cash. Everyone should have approximately one year's living expenses in liquid assets.

- Cash flow: You could have all the money in the world, but don't have it readily available to pay your monthly bills and other obligations, then you and your financial condition are poor.

- Return on net-worth (or equity): Return on net worth is equity or how much you earn on your investments on an annual basis, considering inflation. Is it positive or negative, and it has to be positive to be sustainable.

These four areas hold the keys to your continued financial success in life after you are done working. Most people build their resources through intelligent and analytical thinking, which gives them the option to make choices; these choices are generally more emotional than thoughtful, *so be careful*—this is your financial well-being we are talking about. You may have always wanted a beach house, but think twice before buying one.

B. Organizing your Assets

It is amazing how many people don't know what they have, and where the paperwork that is associated with what they have is located. Thus begins the hard work of organizing paperwork associated with all the accounts, insurance policies, assets, wills, and anything else that you might share with someone if you were not able to be present either physically or mentally. One valuable tool that our financial advisor developed when we first became a client was the "black notebook." We compiled our entire financial history into one place, and it included:

- All banking accounts

- Investments of each and every description, including real estate and personal items

- Insurance policies, including, life, disability, casualty, automobile, umbrella policies, etc.

- Any and all contracts, wills, codicils, trust agreements, and other agreements or legal documents

- All debts and liabilities, including credit card balances and mortgages

We made two copies of the notebook in addition to the originals. We kept the original book and one copy and the financial advisor kept the second complete copy. Our children know where we keep the notebook and who to contact if my wife and I both die suddenly together. Our entire financial life is in the notebook. Of course, it must be updated annually, but it is a comfort to know it is all in one safe place (really, two safe places).

When putting a notebook together, make sure to put it back in a safe location. Preferably, you'd have this information in two safe locations so that in the event of a fire, damaging storm, or anything else that might destroy the first location, you or your loved ones have access to this vital information.

-As you go through your documents, policies, and accounts, ask whether certain items are worth hanging on to. For example, you may have purchased disability insurance, life insurance, or long-term care insurance years ago, but your current circumstances no longer warrant it. As you get older and your assets become greater, you have less of a need for life insurance and disability insurance. In addition, the older you get, the higher the premiums, so the policies might not be worth the added costs. Each individual or family will need to decide which policies are worth keeping. For example, if one spouse has a steady stream of income and he or she dies, the income (disability benefits, a stock buy-out, income from a second career, etc.) is not transferable to the other spouse, so a life insurance policy might be necessary to cover this shortfall.

C. Choosing an Advisory Firm

If you choose to look for an advisory firm, shop for longevity, reputation, and alignment with your needs. Longevity stands out as the best indicator of past and future success. This does not mean that an organization with longevity is the only purveyor of great advice, support, and guidance, but that it has merely been doing it longer than others. It is also wise not to work with an individual advisor who has had fewer than five years of experience.

Reputation is a little harder to discern, but it is important to know the community's perception of the advisory firm that you are about to employ. It is possible to get recommendations from the clients of the prospective firm, and although, these clients will be biased, they will also tell you a lot about the character and flavor of their relationship and communications with your perspective advisory firm.

When you consider that your relationship with an advisory firm is a fiduciary relationship (the firm serves as your advocate) and not an agency relationship (the firm serves as a sales channel), then alignment becomes key. Typically, but not always, advisory firms operate on fee-for-service compensation. However, the compensation is not as important as the competency and alignment of your interests with that individual and firm.

In your first meeting with the firm, you want to establish the "three Cs." That is to say that the firm and the individual financial advisor will work with customers to create value, communicate, and build comfort in the relationship. The following is an explanation of the three Cs:

- Creating value means that you as the client can clearly understand how your advisor can provide a return greater than the cost of services. For example, your advisor might be able to provide an immediate return through tax savings or create value through a longer term investment, but you're not just handing over the reins. In either case, you (the client) would understand how that value (i.e., money) is created.

- Communication is a critical part of the relationship you are trying to build with the advisor. You and the advisor must be able understand what each other is saying. A good advisor is first and foremost a good listener. It is the advisor's responsibility to provide an active, empathic listening environment that is safe for all parties to speak freely and have their concerns heard.

- Comfort is the most difficult concept to explain, but for the long-term relationship, it is the most essential. For you to have truly positive and candid conversations and to feel comfortable handing your finances and legacy to a third party, the elements of trust, empathy, transparency, and a caring are required.

If the process begins to feel more like a prospecting session to see what can be sold, move on and continue your search for the right firm. Be careful with the advisors who will not disclose compensation, commission, transaction costs, service fees, or any other matter you may professionally inquire about.

D. Going it Alone

Unless you are an expert in investments and financial transactions, you may be better served to have a professional direct your investments during retirement. If you do it yourself, you can certainly save a great deal of money, but you may sacrifice your stomach lining and sleep. It all depends on your risk acceptance and risk aversion. Some people are natural gamblers, and several of my friends manage all or some of their funds for the intellectual stimulation as well as the "fun" of it. There is nothing wrong with this approach, but sometimes we tend to have a "hold my beer and watch this" attitude right before we crash.

For those who want to manage their assets on their own, Diesslin recommends studying three major areas: past investment trends, the current investment environment, and what I would call alternative investing and global implications.

While a graduate student at the University of Chicago in the 1950s, Harry Markowitz developed a theory of investing that has become the foundation of financial economics and has revolutionized investment practice[27]. His theory centered around the fact that all investments are based on trade-offs. In other words, there is a limited number of dollars to invest, and one has to decide what percentage should be at risk and what percentage should be completely safe. It helps to visualize a pie chart containing 100% of your investment dollars. If 100 % is invested in government bonds and cash, there is virtually

---

[27] Bernstein, Peter. *Capital Ideas: The Impossible Origins of Modern Wall Street*. The Free Press, New York, 1992.

no risk; if 100 % is invested in small capitalization stocks, then 100% of your dollars are arguably at risk. In simple terms you should not put all your eggs in one basket.

At first, Markowitz's model was populated with individual stocks but has evolved to include portfolios of stocks in individual categories. The diversification is endless, but most portfolio managers rely on large caps, small caps, international markets, bonds, and cash ("cap" stands for capitalization, which implies the size and financial health of the company whose stocks you have purchased). Some add precious metals, currencies, and real estate investment trusts.

You should reevaluate and recalculate the percentages of dollars that are safe and at-risk annually and adjust according to real and perceived risk. Your personal assets must be aligned with your personal risk acceptance. If you cannot stand the thought of ever losing capital, then you should keep your money in low-risk cash and certificates of deposit. Theoretically, the older you get the fewer equities you should own and the more cash, bonds, and certificates of deposit you should accumulate. If you are in your early 60s and in good health, you have some time to be adventuresome, but if your timeline is short, there is safety and comfort in more solid investments that will not fluctuate and give you a steady return. As I stated earlier, I was more comfortable having someone else do the analysis and redistribution on an annual basis, but there is no real reason you cannot do this yourself.

Another approach is to invest in index funds, which are based on owning a percentage of each stock listed in a particular index, such as the Standard and Poor 500, the Russell 2000 (which is small cap companies), and the DJ Wilshire (which based on the entire stock market). There are indexes of bonds, foreign stocks, and others. The advantage to this strategy is that the investment firm holds stock management to a minimum since an index fund is based on a simple percentage or formula, which is all calculated by a computer. Therefore, no one has to make any decisions (and thus, charge you for those decisions).

Again, the above discussion is for educational purposes only and simply to motivate you to explore your options through the help of professional advisors. The core lesson is to create a rational, intelligent, diversified portfolio that conforms to your risk tolerance. Your investing choices hinge on your aversion to risk, your life expectancy, and how well you want to sleep at night.

Chapter Ten
PIDDLING, POTHOLES, AND PEARLS

"Nothing is more difficult and therefore more precious, than to be able to decide."

Napoleon Bonaparte (1769-1821)

I have always suffered from "tyranny of the urgent." I was always looking for things to do, places to go, projects to start, books to write, what to do next. Freedom was really a frightening prospect for me. I suspect for many of us, as illustrated by the candid stories of my friends, that I am not alone in my fear. Although I urge you to get involved in your community and find productive ways to occupy your time, I also encourage you to take time to be unproductive as well. In this chapter, I hope to summarize the essence of this book, which is to enjoy your freedom in the next stage of your journey.

A. Piddle Away a Few Hours a Week

Piddle has a couple of meanings. Brewster, my Boykin Spaniel bird dog, likes to piddle. He really enjoys "marking his territory," thus he is a piddler. This is not how I suggest you spend your time. Rather, let's follow the other definition of the word, which is to spend time in a wasteful, trifling, or ineffectual way. There is a place and a time for piddling, and it always serves a purpose. Piddling is relaxing. You don't get paid for it, or at least you shouldn't. You don't piddle with a time constraint, and you don't really enjoy the fruits of piddling. Piddling can be a healthy pursuit. You could wax your boat, even if it doesn't need it. You could whittle something out of wood with no general purpose in mind. Fishing is not piddling, but rearranging your tackle box is. Piddling is shopping for stuff you don't need, especially if you come home empty handed. You don't need an education to piddle; in fact, the more education you have, the more difficult it is to piddle. Piddling probably has started more spousal arguments than anything else, with the exception of money. One spouse sees the other piddling and wonders what on earth he or she is wasting time on. The piddler defends his piddling, and the argument begins. Piddling is personal and is yours alone. That is the secret. All of us should take the time to piddle; it clears the mind, helps purge your type A compulsive nature, and in the long run, probably helps you live longer.

B. Avoid Potholes

You're bound to hit many potholes as you enter retirement. Some are well marked, some you don't notice until you hit them. Lack of planning leads to potholes, and it can be expensive and time consuming to repair the damage. They can make us stronger or ruin our tires. Self-pity can turn into a deep pothole if you're not careful. Feeling sorry for yourself may get you some attention in the short-term, but the negative force it creates is not worth it. If you are still on this side of the flowers, be thankful. My mother has defied the odds for years. She has congestive heart failure, pulmonary fibrosis, a complete heart blockage, and atrial fibrillation. She lived completely independently until she had a stroke at 92. She has had a remarkable recovery thanks to the excellent physical, speech, and occupational therapists.

On her 93rd birthday, I asked her what she had been doing, and she said, "Nothing, and I don't start that until noon." She could have launched into a soliloquy of self-pity over the loss of her independence, her health issues, and her age, but she instead chose to laugh hard and long over her wisecrack. I truly hope I have that perspective when and if I am that old.

Another pothole is spending an inordinate amount of time worrying about the state of affairs and the affairs of state. No matter your political bent, everything seems to be going in the wrong direction. You can ruin a perfectly good day by reading the newspaper (I read three every day). Agonizing over what you have very little or no control is not worth the energy. If the cause or issue is important to you, vote, volunteer, contribute, blog, but don't just sit there and tell everyone that the world is going to hell. Believe me; no one wants to hear it.

Regret is another pothole that you're bound to hit if you don't steer carefully. Settle past conflicts and disagreements. Apologize and move on. A hateful heart is not a healthy heart. Those people who are isolated and angry don't live as long as those who are surrounded by family and friends and have faith in something greater than themselves. Put the past behind you, stay in the present. The deepest pothole is probably inactivity. Physical, mental, and spiritual inactivity will age you faster than time.

C. Aubrey and Barbara Guthrie's Story: Sharing Pearls of Wisdom

Aubrey Guthrie, MD, retired at the age of 65 because he was fed up with being told how and when to practice medicine. He is now 79. His father and his grandfather were both family physicians, and his father practiced until he was 86. Aubrey's dad could not understand why he retired so young. Barbara Guthrie, RN, BS, PhD, was a school nurse and educator in public schools in underserved areas for her entire career. She is now 74. She decided at age 50 to pursue a PhD in literature. Her thesis was entitled *C. S. Lewis; Spiritual Quest and Health*.

Aubrey, Barbara, and I discussed many things, and their collective wisdom was enlightening. They posited that you must spend your pre-retirement days preparing for what you are going to do next. Here are a few of their pearls:

- Journal daily. Write what you felt, what you thought, and your impressions of things and people, not what you did.
- Follow a spiritual path. Aubrey and Barbara structured their spiritual life through the Episcopal Church, and they spent time in meditation and reflection. Both of them mutually studied the life and words of the Dali Lama.
- Surround yourself with interesting people with whom you can discuss real issues and thoughts in-depth. They did this both individually and as a couple.
- Stay in nature. Aubrey and Barbara spend a great deal of time outside. They traveled the country in an RV spending time in the woods and by the water, appreciating the solitude of nature and what it has to offer.

- Read, read, and read. Barbara and Aubrey both read extensively, fiction and nonfiction. "It is important to have something to THINK about," they said.

- Have a hobby. Despite his color blindness, Aubrey is a master photographer and has won numerous awards for this work. He continues to explore new techniques. Barbara helps him "see" the color. Barbara's hobby is helping others. She lives for the opportunity to help and is a gifted "keeper of wisdom."

- Help others. Aubrey and Barbara help others navigate the "medical maze," by directing them to the right professionals and by physically taking them, staying with them, and interpreting what the physicians recommend. Aubrey quoted the Dali Lama: "It makes one's existence by being useful and helpful to other people."

After 54 years of marriage, Aubrey and Barbara both enjoy each other's company but enjoy their time alone. Aubrey's advice for those who are about to retire is to "give up your role." Be prepared to retire and "get a life." Remember to focus on the *being* part of human being.

D. You Can't Get a Butterfly by Stapling Wings to a Worm

Retirement will be a struggle for many, and for some, finding happiness in retirement will take some inner work. In other words, rather than waiting for the external forces of your life to change, you may need to change what is on the inside. I use the story of the butterfly to motivate those struggling with addiction to remain in recovery. You can't get a butterfly by stapling wings to a worm. The butterfly, as you know, is a worm first. It builds a chrysalis and becomes completely liquefied while the DNA is rearranged into a butterfly. It is a true transformational change from within.

There are three key points to this transformation. First, the butterfly has to completely give up being a worm—it can never go back. Second, the chrysalis has to be firmly anchored to withstand the forces of nature. Third, if the butterfly did not have to struggle to get out of the chrysalis, it would fall to the ground unable to fly. If we change just because someone else thinks we should, then it is usually not permanent and long lasting. The strength comes from the struggle. Some of the toughest people I know are those who have struggled to get to where they are in life.

E. Finding Pearls

When I attend a lecture or read a book, I am always looking for a few pearls of wisdom to take away with me. Many times, I have suffered through hours of instruction and couldn't find the pearls. Each of us interprets these pieces of information and wisdom differently; what I think of as a pearl, you may think is a lump of coal. What was a pearl 40 years ago may not be a pearl today. Our personalities, experience, knowledge, relationships, and place in time determine our pearls. The following are a list of my pearls that I have collected over the years and some that I have borrowed from friends. Pick out a few of the following pearls to live by and make some new ones of your own:

- Be kind to everyone

- Remember, we are all struggling, so treat everyone with empathy and respect
- Try not to judge; be tolerant, but don't forsake your values
- Make your spouse your partner
- Share
- Don't let someone else determine your happiness
- Write something
- Read something
- Teach
- Build something
- Create something for someone else
- Challenge yourself, not others
- Get outside your comfort zone by learning a language, how to fly a plane, or to dance
- If you have been fortunate to have a long-time spouse, thank him or her for putting up with you
- Cultivate friendships
- Pay it forward
- Perform an random act of kindness
- Give things away

- Try not to worry about things you have no control over
- Enjoy the birds and flowers
- Listen to others
- Remember that your legacy maybe unintended
- Practice being alone; solitude is good for the soul
- Get a dog or a cat
- You will not be happy if you lose your options, so stay healthy
- Thank the people who helped you along the way
- Be truly thankful for every day
- Laugh, especially at yourself
- Exercise your body, mind, and soul
- Love

When you find yourself struggling to find your way during retirement, remember the story of the small lantern: a Christian missionary in the darkest of nights in the Congo heard a noise at the window of her hut and found a tribal elder standing outside, holding a very small lamp. The elder had risked his life walking through a very dangerous area to deliver a message to the missionary. "Such a pathetic light on such a dark night," the missionary said. "It shines as far as I can step," the elder replied. Retirement may seem like a great darkness where fear and anxiety lurk, but no one can possibly know what will happen in the next hour or the next day. Stay in the present.

CPSIA information can be obtained at www.ICGtesting.com
Printed in the USA
BVOW041929110213

312971BV00001B/145/P